LIVING MIRRORS
Reflecting the Image of God

Other Books by the Same Author
(Writing as A.G. Hill)

- The Song of the Seraphim Chronicles: George and the Monster Inside.

- The Song of the Seraphim Chronicles: George and the Sinister Shadow.

- **Contact author by visiting andrewghill1958.uk**

Andrew G Hill

LIVING

MIRRORS

Reflecting the Image of God

Dedication

This book is dedicated to the memory of my wife, Joyce.
A living mirror of her Saviour Christ Jesus.

Contents

The Aims of this Book

I cannot remember the name of the first Christian book I read but I do remember being baffled by the complex language the author used. The problem with most books looking at Christian teaching is that they assume that the reader has some knowledge of the subject, but me, just starting out on my Christian life, reading, and understanding the Bible was hard enough without trying to wade through a book of doctrinal terms I had never heard of before.

The inclusion of Bible references within the text also baffled me. I would spend ages searching for the reference in the Bible, only to lose the thread of the book I was reading. The references were abbreviated, and again, I had no idea what the abbreviations meant especially as there was no explanation of them, so I wrote this book for those who have just started out on their Christian life and are not familiar with technical terms. It is also for those who have been Christians for years but are put off by complex theological language. I try to avoid using technical terms and Christian jargon. Primarily I am referring to words coined by the theologians and scholars; words that are not always found in the pages of the Bible. For example, when I first came across the word, omnipotent, I not only struggled to know how to pronounce it, but I also had no idea what it meant so I had to put the book down and look up the word in a dictionary. Though that can be especially useful and helpful in enlarging the reader's vocabulary, it can also be distracting and off-putting. Omnipotent means all-powerful, so I simply say that. But there are other terms impossible to avoid because they are found in the Bible itself, so I will endeavour to explain them as simply and clearly as I can.

This is a book by an ordinary bloke, for ordinary folk about the extraordinary God and how He transforms our lives. It is written in an informal, conversational style that will, hopefully, be of use to youth groups, home groups and to anyone who is not a professor of theology, though if you are, I hope you enjoy the book too. I have tried to look at a great subject in a practical way that would encourage the reader to grow in their faith. And if you are not a Christian but are 'searching for answers,' then this book is also for you.

I have printed the Bible references in full, so as not to interrupt the flow of the text. The passage is printed in **bold** type to highlight the fact it is a quote from the Bible. I am mainly using the New International Version, Anglicised 1984 edition. Where I have used a different version, I have indicated that. All emphasis in the Bible quotations are mine.

The Bible was written in Hebrew, Aramaic and Greek. The English versions we have are translations. It is often helpful to know what the original word meant, especially as more than one English word can be used to convey the meaning. Sometimes one word, such as love, has four original words in Greek, so it is good to know which word is being used. However, as with all theological works, there is a danger of getting caught up in an intellectual exercise and forgetting that the purpose of the Bible is to introduce us to God. Except for love and the name of God, I have chosen to say what the original word meant rather than tell you what it is. If you do want to find that out, the IVP Bible Dictionary is an excellent resource as are many study Bibles and commentaries.

The Bible is God's word. By that I mean that God not only speaks to us today through the Bible's pages, but He also guided the human writers to put on record what He wanted said. **All Scripture is God-breathed...** (2 Timothy 3:16) **...men spoke from God as they were carried along by the Holy Spirit.** (2 Peter 1:21) The words spirit and breath are the same in the original language and so, 'God-breathed' is another way of saying that the Bible is inspired by God's Spirit. He breathed into or filled the writers with His Spirit, and He revealed the truth to them, while at the same time, allowing the authors to use their own minds and experiences.

Although there were about 40 different authors who lived, in some cases hundreds of years apart from each other, and they came from varied backgrounds; the 66 books of the Bible read as one book with one theme and the 'voice' of one author. God stamped His authority over the Bible. It is a book, in its original text, without error.

When JB Phillips translated the New Testament back in the 1940s, he became convinced that the Bible was no ordinary book and wrote of his experience as a translator in a book called, 'The Ring of Truth.' Phillips spoke of being conscious of a greater author overseeing the words and giving them a living quality that rang true as authentic words of God. When you read the Bible, you need to pray that God will give you understanding so that you 'hear' His voice speaking to you today.

In the book of Acts in the New Testament (NT) there is the account of a group of people who, after hearing the Apostle Paul preaching, searched the Bible to see if what he said was correct. (Incidentally, they searched the Old Testament because the New Testament had not been written by then). **Now the Bereans... received the message with great eagerness and examined the Scriptures every day to see if what Paul said was true.** (Acts 17:11) This is why you will find a lot of Bible quotations in this book and I hope that my words will be weighed up and checked for accuracy by God's word.

The references to the Bible are printed as above, Acts is the book, and 17 is the chapter number. The colon (:) indicates the verse or verses, which in this example, is verse 11.

When I was a boy in primary school many years ago, I was taught that whenever we referred to God, we should use capital letters for personal pronouns. This was, as the teacher explained to us, a mark of respect to God. Sadly, the practise is dying out, but I use capitals for all personal pronouns when referring to the Deity. For copyright reasons, there are exceptions with the quotations from translations that do not capitalise personal pronouns of the Deity.

Acknowledgements

Thank you to Clifford Kitson for professionally, editing the text, you made it better. And to Nelson and Mark Smith for typesetting into a printable format. Your help has been greatly apricated! I also want to thank those who have read the manuscript, given their valuable opinion and patiently suggested changes where necessary: Pastor Robert Hamilton, Steven Hamilton, Dr Jeremy McQuoid, Pastor John Merson, Kit, and my patient wife, Joyce. And also Andy Jack and Micheal Cordiner for checking the proofs. And many others who have given help and encouragement – you know who you are! And thanks to Charlene Cheesman for the amazing cover.

Finally, my prayer is that God will overcome the failings of my writing and that this book will glorify Him and be an encouragement to you to be a living mirror, reflecting the image of God in your day-to-day life.

Introduction: The Mirror Cracked

Made in God's image

The Bible makes an astounding pronouncement on human nature: human beings are meant to be God-like. We are not accidents of evolution, mere animals existing for no apparent reason in a meaningless universe. We do not have to fill the world we live in with violence. Human beings were never meant to murder, hate, cheat, or be at war with each other or greedily destroy the environment. Humans are not evolved savages but were created perfect beings that were never meant to die.

A simple statement is made in the first book of the Bible, the book of Genesis. It states that human beings were *created.* We were designed and put together by a Supreme Being, whom we call God. And God made us to be like Him, so we could share a perfect friendship with Him. **So God created man in His own image, in the image of God he created him; male and female He created them.** (Genesis 1:27)

This does not mean that God looks like us; this is not a physical image but a spiritual one reflecting the character of God. He made us to be living, breathing, walking, talking mirrors reflecting all His goodness and love. We were also made to live forever in perfect harmony with our creator and His world.

When I was writing this book, a leaflet came through my door inviting me to join the humanist society. I read with interest what this group of atheists believe in. The leaflet stated that to be truly human means to live without God, who they see as an obsolete and irrelevant idea, that has no place in an enlightened society. Their aim is to do away with religion, which they see as a negative influence in the world. I will not be joining them because I believe that to be truly human means to enjoy a friendship with God. The origin of the word, religion, is derived from the word relationship. True religion is not a philosophy dreamed up by intellectuals or primitive superstitious people; it is a relationship with the Supreme Person. By sharing this relationship as God intended it to be shared, humans find fulfilment and real purpose in life.

The reality of sin

Humanists believe that we human beings are essentially good and there is no such thing as sin. They explain acts of violence, immorality and crime as a result of being evolved from the savage. Moral decline is blamed on a lack of education, poor housing, bad upbringing and mental health conditions. Political correctness has blurred the distinctions of right and wrong, good and bad, light and dark, black and white. Instead, we are supposed to speak of

18

'shades of grey' because, in the view of secularists, there is no absolute wrong and no absolute right. We are not meant to talk of 'bad behaviour' but 'challenging behaviour.' This is the result of secular society trying to get rid of the concept of sin – secularists deny its very existence. Sin is an unpopular word and it is seen as something outdated (even by some who claim to be Christians).

The Bible, however, is realistic and you cannot escape the word sin when you read it. Sin explains the reality that we are not perfect as we were first created to be. Sin is a word that translates many different words in the Hebrew and Greek, sometimes these words, such as godlessness are used in English Bibles. Looking at the original words, we can get a fuller understanding of what sin is. Sin is to fall short: **all have sinned and fall short of the glory of God...** (Romans 3:23). Missing the mark is another way of saying the same thing. We will look at what it is humans have fallen from and what target they have missed below. Psalm 51 contains this prayer: **...blot out my transgressions. Wash away my iniquity...** (Psalm 51:1, 2) Transgression refers to breaking a specific law and iniquity literally means lawlessness**... sin is lawlessness.** (1 John 3:4). Sin is godlessness: **"See, the Lord is coming with thousands upon thousands of his holy ones to judge everyone, and to convict all the ungodly of all the ungodly acts they have done in the ungodly way, and of all the harsh words ungodly sinners have spoken against him."** (Jude 14, 15) Other root words and phrases for sin are: to trespass, to do wrong, to hurt, to be in debt to God, disobedience, injustice and dishonesty.

We see a pattern emerging, which is that sin is against God. **Against you, you only, have I sinned and done what is evil in your sight...** (Psalm 51:4). In essence, sin is rebellion against God and all that He represents. It is anything that is contrary to what is good and holy. It is to be independent of God and do things our own way and to be totally self-centred. Sin is not just a deed, but an attitude and a condition of humanity. Genesis chapter three not only records the first sin but also gives us an idea of its nature.

The origin of sin and the Fall of man

Genesis one and two describe a world created as perfect. The word 'good' appears seven times in the first chapter. God made a good world without any fault. And He made mankind perfect as well. Part of that perfection was to share in the glory of God by reflecting all His goodness. God's presence was tangible, Adam and Eve could see God and experienced a deep friendship with Him. The glory of God was also shared by being placed as the highest of all that God had created, giving the man and the woman the responsibility of ruling over the world with God. **God said to them... "Rule over the fish of the sea and the birds of the air and over every living creature that moves on the ground."** (Genesis 1: 28)

Another aspect of perfection is to possess free will. Love is a choice, not a programme downloaded to a mindless computer. God made man with the ability to choose. This is shown by God making an agreement with Adam, the first man. He is the representative of all men and women upon the earth. The agreement was that God would provide everything for Adam and he would look after the rest of creation. God provided a companion, the woman, Eve, thus creating the template for marriage. Man and woman would become physically, spiritually and emotionally one in sexual union. **This is why a man leaves his father and mother and bonds with his wife, and they become one flesh.** (Genesis 2:24 HCSB)

When a person is in love, they seek to please the object of their love by doing things for them. God gave all that Adam and Eve needed and they, in turn, agreed to do whatever God asked of them. As a sign of their agreement, God used a tree as a symbol of trust between them. To demonstrate his love for God, Adam agreed not to eat the fruit of the tree. Let's clear up a misunderstanding here. The tree was not an apple tree. There is no mention of apples in Genesis three. People added to the Bible story and speculated that Adam ate an apple but the tree symbolised knowledge that only God possesses and can handle – the knowledge of what is good and what is evil – in other words, all knowledge. To disobey God would be evil because it would be a betrayal of His love and trust. To obey God would show how much Adam and Eve loved God in return. God was their creator and king – He has absolute authority – He alone decides what good and what is evil and to disobey Him is to reject that authority. It is to say, "I am my own king and I alone decide what I can and cannot do."

The Bible makes it clear that God has an enemy. The name Satan literally means, 'adversary'. In Hebrew, he is '*The* Satan' = 'The Adversary.' There are clues in the Bible as to his origin but no definite account. He was one of the angels of God, indeed, the chief angel. But though created a supernatural being, he wanted to *be* God and led a rebellion in Heaven leading to the expulsion of many angels. This adversary is symbolised as a serpent: **The great dragon was hurled down – that ancient serpent called the devil, or Satan, who leads the whole world astray.** (Revelation 12: 9)

In Genesis 3, we read of The Satan's successful temptation of Adam and Eve: **"You will not surely die," the serpent said to the woman, "For God knows that when you eat of it your eyes will be opened, and you will be like God, knowing good and evil." When the woman saw that the fruit of the tree was... desirable for gaining wisdom, she took some and ate it. She also gave some to her husband, who was with her, and he ate it.** (Genesis 3:5-6)

The enemy suggested that humans could possess wisdom or all knowledge. He tempted them to live an independent life without God and be in total control of their own destiny. The temptation was to replace God as the ruler and Supreme Being, for only He is all-knowing and all-powerful. Did you notice that Adam was with his wife at the time The Satan was tempting her? **She also gave some to her husband, who was with her, and he ate it.** Sadly, he was silent and made no attempt to stop Eve from listening to The Satan's lies. Why? Because he too was enticed by the idea of being wise in his own eyes, of possessing knowledge only God possessed, of being his own god. From being God-centred, Adam and Eve were becoming self-centred. Their love for God had been eclipsed by love for themselves. The moment they disobeyed, both died spiritually. Mankind's ability to know God intimately was ruined by that act of rebellion. The human spirit was no longer able to cope with the glory of the Almighty. The relationship Adam was totally dependent upon for life, had now been broken, and eventually, he would die physically too.

This account of the first act of sin is termed as 'the fall of man'. Tripping over and falling can be dangerous, it can result in injury or even death. The old saying that 'the higher you are, the harder you will fall' is especially true of Adam – he fell from the glory of God! He fell from perfection. He fell from that perfect friendship and became an enemy of God. He fell from God's high standard and missed the mark of God's goodness. The shiny new mirror now had man's dirty fingerprints all over it. It was cracked and the image distorted like the grotesque reflections seen in the mirrors at fairgrounds. From that point on human nature was not as God intended it to be. Because Adam was the representative of all mankind, every human being since then has been born with a sinful, rebellious nature at war with its Creator. **...for all have sinned and fall short of the glory of God...** (Romans 3:23) Sin is a virus invading our systems, upsetting the perfect balance, destroying our health and distorting our very personalities. Like a virus, it has spread through every generation to the present day. Humans are not naturally good because we have all inherited Adam's sinful nature. But the good news of the Bible is that God did not leave it at that.

The perfect mirror

At the moment mankind sinned, God announced His rescue plan. Speaking to Satan, God said: **"And I will put enmity between you and the woman, and between your off-spring and hers; he will crush your head, and you will strike his heel."** (Genesis 3:15) This is the first promise of a Rescuer or Saviour – one who would rescue everyone from sin and evil. This man born of a woman would be the crusher of the serpent, but He would suffer a fatal wound as He rescued us. The rest of the Bible begins to trace this promise, which is fulfilled in the person of Jesus Messiah. We will be looking at how Jesus fulfilled this promise in more detail later when we examine His death and resurrection.

God would not only save mankind from sin and evil, but He would also restore His image within human beings. He would do so through the One who would be the perfect representative of mankind and the perfect representative of God. Jesus Messiah is the perfect mirror of God the Father's image; a living mirror that could never become tarnished or distorted or cracked.

He is the image of the invisible God... (Colossians 1:15) **The Son is the radiance of God's glory and the exact representation of his being, sustaining all things by his powerful word** (Hebrews 1:3). If we want to know what God is like, then all we need do is look at Jesus because He reveals God to us. That's not all though, He also reveals to us what a human being is meant to be. Here was a man without sin, living in complete obedience and perfect harmony with God His Father.

We become truly human and fulfilled when we are like Jesus, for then we will be what God originally created us to be: God-like and His image bearers. Becoming like Jesus is what this book is all about. It is an attempt to explain how Christians are transformed into living mirrors bearing the image of God that is being restored in them. Becoming like Jesus is a life-long process, but we will not be perfect and completely free from sin this side of Heaven. The process is completed when we enter Heaven and into God's wonderful presence.

This book is divided into two parts. The first part looks at God, asking in effect, who is God? If we are to be His image bearers it will be helpful to know who God is and what He is like. The second part looks at the work of the Holy Spirit in the believer's life, asking in effect, how do we reflect God's image? This section will examine in some detail what is known as the fruit of the Spirit from Galatians chapter 5.

PART ONE: Who GOD IS

Chapter One

The Incomprehensible, Personal, Spirit

Peeking behind the curtain

The Temple in Jerusalem was a magnificent structure admired by all the Jews. All that remains of it now are the foundations and the western wall, known as the Wailing Wall, because devout Jews pray and weep beside it. In the days of its splendour, the sanctuary was divided in two by a massive curtain. One part of the sanctuary was called the Holy Place and the other, behind the curtain, was called the Holy of Holies or the Most Holy Place. Behind this curtain was a golden box, called the Ark of the Covenant, containing the Ten Commandments given by God to Moses. The only person allowed to enter the Most Holy Place was the high priest, and even then, only once a year. This is because that part of the sanctuary represented Heaven on earth, where God would meet the representative of His people, and sinful man cannot simply barge into the presence of the Holy One.

To look at God is to enter the Holy of Holies, and so we must enter with humility and caution. Our look at God is more of a peek behind the curtain rather than a long gaze, for this book is not big enough to explore in-depth such a massive subject. When Isaiah, the priest saw the glory of God, he was awestruck: **"Woe is me!" I cried. "I am ruined! For I am a man of unclean lips, and I live among a people of unclean lips, and my eyes have seen the King, the LORD Almighty."** (Isaiah 6:5)

Looking at who God is should put us in the place of humble admiration and obedience. God is awesome – an overused word in danger of losing its impact – it means that something or someone fills you with fear mixed with wonder. God is so overwhelmingly powerful and glorious that we are lost for words when we realise just how insignificant we are compared to Him. Isaiah felt his own sinfulness and cried for mercy. It is easy to compare ourselves with other people; we can always be selective and believe we are a better person because we see a fault in them that we think we don't have. (They will see a fault in us that they think they don't have!) But nothing and no one can compare with Almighty God. Peeking behind the curtain at the glory of God will make us aware of our own littleness and sinfulness. You have been warned.

It takes a lifetime to really look at God and there is a sense of futility in trying to describe who He is because the subject is so beyond us, so "other". As He puts it Himself:

As the heavens (sky/universe) **are higher than the earth, so are my ways higher than your ways, and my thoughts than your thoughts.** (Isaiah 55:9) It is presumptuous of us to think that we can answer the question: who is God, what is He like? We can only get a glimpse of His glory, for our minds can never fully grasp the mysteries of His Being.

The good news is that we can consider what God has revealed to us about Himself. This is what Biblical Christianity affirms: it is a revealed religion. What we know of God is what He Himself has shown to us. The purpose of Bible study is not to critique the book but to receive the revelation. Our peek at God consists of a digest of the attributes of God. Put simply, the attributes of God are the characteristics of His nature as shown by Him. They are a description of who God is. This is the Biblical picture of God and not a picture painted by philosophers or other religions. Some attributes will take longer to look at than others, so the following chapters will be a little uneven in length.

God is beyond our understanding

The first thing we need to grasp (as I have already stated) is that we will never understand God. We need to accept that there are some questions we will never be able to answer. God is unlike anything we can ever imagine. If you think of it logically, this is part of what makes God who He is. If we could understand Him, fully explain Him to our complete satisfaction, He would cease to be the Supreme Being and be no more than the product of our imagination. The only person who ever understood God is God!

When you read the accounts of the life of Jesus Christ in Matthew, Mark, Luke, and John, you discover that His disciples were baffled by Him. Many of His ways and sayings were beyond them. Their inability to understand Jesus was due to the fact that He is divine. It took over three years for them to realise that Jesus was more than a man, and this was only after the Spirit of God revealed the truth to them. An incident in John's gospel illustrates this point. One of the disciples asked Jesus to show God to them and **Jesus answered: "Don't you know me, Philip, even after I have been among you such a long time? Anyone who has seen me has seen the Father. How can you say, 'Show us the Father'? Don't you believe that I am in the Father, and that the Father is in me?"** (John 14:9)

To get a glimpse of God, we need to look at Jesus because it is via Jesus that we connect to God the Father. Through Jesus, we can know the Father personally, but even then, we will not understand Him or work out His ways. You cannot put God in a box or under a microscope. Our minds are finite – tiny, limited – He is infinite – limitless and bigger than the whole universe, beyond all human understanding. The best thing is not to try to comprehend Him – He is too big so don't bother – just accept the fact that He is. This is essentially what Paul does at the end of his doctrinal teaching from Romans 1-11. Paul has been exploring the deep things of God, the nature of salvation, and His sovereign right to do with us what He wishes. There are things Paul writes that are hard to understand and he knows this; he too is overwhelmed with the subject so he bursts into a song of praise:

Oh, the depth of the riches of the wisdom

and knowledge of God!

How unsearchable his judgments, and

his paths beyond tracing out!

"Who has known the mind of the Lord?

Or who has been his counsellor?

Who has ever given to God, that God

should repay him?"

For from him and through him and

to him are all things.

To him be the glory forever! Amen

(Romans 11:33-36)

We need to remind ourselves of this whenever the head hurts trying to grasp the majesty of God. As we continue in our peek at God, we will encounter many incomprehensible things, but that's okay because being beyond our understanding is part of who God is.

God is Spirit

This means quite simply that God is not limited by a body. He has no physical form. Though we often describe God as being big, this is referring to the idea or Person of God rather than any physical size. The idea made popular in art,

33

of God being an old man with a long white beard, is completely false and is influenced by pagan beliefs, particularly Greek mythology, and its portrait of Zeus.

When the Bible does use physical features to describe God, such as His powerful right arm, His eye, face, or back, it is using terms that will help us understand the concept being conveyed by a particular passage. For example, God's 'right arm' refers to His power and His 'eye' simply means that He sees. When we are told that God spoke to Moses face to face, this is referring to the closeness of their relationship because Moses could not look at God's face.

In Exodus 33:19-22, Moses asks to see God's glory. **He said, "I will cause My goodness to pass in front of you, and I will proclaim the name Yahweh before you. You cannot see My face, for no one can see Me and live... I will put you in the crevice of the rock and cover you with My hand until I have passed by. Then I will take My hand away, and you will see My back, but My face will not be seen."** (Exodus 33:19-22, HCSB) This does give the impression that God has a body but then we read that: **The LORD came down in a cloud, stood with him there, and proclaimed His name Yahweh.** (Exodus 34:5, HCSB)

There are several instances where God appears in a cloud and a cloud has no form because it is made of vapour. What Moses saw was God's majestic Glory. But Moses did not see all of God's Glory, just His "back" – a glimpse of glory – because His Glory is so great that to see it fully would have caused Moses's sinful nature to turn to dust because holiness blots out sin completely.

The effect of seeing God caused Moses's face to literally shine, creating fear in those who saw him, creating the idea of intense light. **God is light; in him, there is no darkness at all.** (1 John 1:5) Although light and darkness are used frequently in the Bible as symbols for good and evil, the Bible writers often describe God as being brighter than the sun in full strength, so there must be a literal brilliance to God's Glory.

It is difficult for us to imagine a Being who is Spirit without any physical form and when we do, we can get tangled up in all kinds of wrong images, especially when we come across a description of God having wings. **"May you be richly rewarded by the LORD, the God of Israel, under whose wings you have come to take refuge."** (Ruth 2:12) This description of wings is a word picture to suggest a quality of God. In this example, the quality of a protector and comforter, like a parent bird protecting their young.

Generally, we have no difficulties in understanding the use of metaphors in the Bible. We realise that when Jesus compares Himself to an object by saying He is, for example, the Bread of life; we know that He is not literally a loaf of bread, but just as bread nourishes us and gives life, so He gives spiritual life to those who trust Him. We need to use our intelligence in working out what is meant when the Bible uses a physical description of the Almighty. Any physical descriptions of God are illustrations, mainly to convey the fact that God is a person.

However, there are one or two physical appearances of God in the Bible... Jesus said, **"I am the light of the**

world." (John 9:5) He is the One who reveals God the Father to us and this has always been the case, even before He was born. Abraham was sitting by his tent one day when three strangers came to him. He invited them to rest and provided a meal for them. It soon became apparent that these were no ordinary men. Two of them were angels, and one is clearly God because He is referred to as the LORD. When the three visitors are about to depart, the LORD reveals His intention of destroying the evil city of Sodom. **The men turned away and went toward Sodom, but Abraham remained standing before the LORD.** (Genesis 18:22) Later on, the two men who left are called angels, but the person who stays with Abraham is God Himself.

This is actually an appearance of God the Son. When speaking to the religious leaders of His day, Jesus said, **"Your father Abraham rejoiced at the thought of seeing my day; he saw it and was glad... I tell you the truth... before Abraham was born, I am!"** (John 8:56, 58) It was God the Son before He was born as a human, who appeared to Abraham, Moses, Isaiah, and others. However, He did not appear in His full Glory but as a man.

"God is Spirit." (John 4:24) The original words for spirit in Hebrew and Greek are the same as the words for air, wind, and breath. When God breathed into Adam, He gave him a living spirit. You cannot see air, wind, or breath. They have no form, but you can see what they affect, like the leaves of a tree blown about by a storm. Air keeps us alive; it is powerful enough to run a road drill or lift an aeroplane. The Holy Spirit keeps us alive, makes us alive to spiritual things and is more powerful than we can ever imagine.

God is a person

Frequently in this book, I have referred to God as a person. This fact sets God apart from being abstract and distant, a list of mind-boggling attributes. He is a person who can be known, not a thing, an influence, or an idea. God communicates, and that suggests an intelligent Being, someone who thinks. God has feelings, He can be grieved, and He takes delight in His creation. God demonstrates His power – He acts and breaks into our world. God is alive. **"You are the Christ, the Son of the *living* God."** (Matthew 16:16,)

And this is true of God the Father, God the Son, and God the Holy Spirit. Jesus referred to them as "He" never "it". **And I will ask the Father, and *he* will give you another Counsellor to be with you forever – the Spirit of truth. The world cannot accept *him*, because it neither sees *him* nor knows *him*. But you know *him*, for *he* lives with you and will be in you.** (John 14:16-17) This is a personal Being, who becomes so close that He lives in the heart of a true Christian. This is someone we can talk to; tell Him our concerns, fears, worries, joys, hopes, and dreams. This Person is a friend and a father. He cares, He loves, He provides, and He is with us when all others forsake us. He became a man in Jesus precisely so that we could share an eternal personal friendship with Him.

He or She?

Atheists like to stir up a controversy now and again when they say, 'Why do you suppose that God is a *he* and not a *she?*'. This statement is designed to ridicule and confuse believers, so I will attempt an answer. The fact is that the Bible – the book inspired by God – reveals God as 'He'. Jesus, as I have said, called God Father and He is the Son and He used the male personal pronoun when speaking of the Holy Spirit. That should be the end of the matter. Sadly, there are those in the church who say that because God is Spirit, He is neither male nor female, so it's okay to call God she! They argue that some passages in the Bible suggest that God has a feminine side: ... **how often I have longed to gather your children together, as a hen gathers her chicks under her wings...** (Luke 13:34) **As a mother comforts her child, so will I comfort you...** (Isaiah 66:13) On the strength of these and other references, some in the church have attempted to re-write the Lord's Prayer with 'Our Father/Mother in Heaven.' But the verses quoted above are comparisons conveying the fact that God cares deeply.

It is dangerous and blasphemous to change the Lord's Prayer and start calling God she because it goes beyond the Bible's revelation of God. To present God as anything other than He has presented Himself in the Bible, is to deny the truth and be guilty of idolatry. Some argue that because fathers have abused children, it is helpful to use mother instead, but this makes no sense because some mothers have abused children too. Another argument is that the Bible is a product of its time and it reflects a patriarchal society.

Men were in charge, so they used the male gender to reflect their superior view of themselves. That can be easily answered in the following way.

The Israelites were called out of paganism. Abraham was a pagan living in Ur in Babylonia and later in Harran before God revealed Himself and led him to Canaan. Not only did people worship the sun, moon, and stars, but they also worshipped the earth, which is always presented as female – Mother Earth. Evidence that the Babylonian moon god had a wife called Ningal, has been found in the remains of temples at Ur and Harran. There were many female deities, including Ishtar the goddess of love, and Aya, the wife of the god Shamash. This was the pagan world and this man Abraham forsook that world and worshipped the God who is addressed as He – despite the culture of the day.

Abraham's descendants, the Israelites, were led out of Egypt with its worship of various gods including Isis, the wife of Osiris, Hathor the goddess of joy, and Nekhbet, the vulture-goddess. The culture the Israelites left had female deities and the culture of the peoples of the land they were being led to, also had their fertility goddess. The LORD commanded them to be separate from those religions and wipe out any trace of idolatry. **Break down their altars, smash their sacred stones and burn their Asherah poles in the fire...** (Deuteronomy 12: 3). Asherah was a Canaanite mother-goddess. What marked the people of Israel from all the other cultures around them was their insistence on worshipping this one God, referred to as 'He.'

The followers of Jesus Christ were also different in worshipping this one God and insisting on male personal pronouns even though Roman and Greek cultures had many gods and goddesses. What can be the reason for these ancient believers to go against the culture of the day? It can only be a revelation; this is how God has chosen to be known. The God of the Bible is God. He is a Person whom, through faith in Jesus Christ, we can call Father.

Chapter Two

The Unique Three Persons

in One

God is one

We have seen that despite the culture of the time, the ancient Jews and first Christians believed in one God. True faith in God is always counter-cultural – it goes against the flow of popular worldly views and practices. There is no other God but the God of the Bible, this one Supreme Being did not arise from the human mind but from His own revelation. All other ideas of God, particularly multiple gods and goddesses are inventions of men. That is not a politically correct thing to say, but it is the teaching of the Bible and the true Christian position. We believe in one God and not in many gods. **"Hear, O Israel: The LORD our God, the LORD is one."** (Deuteronomy 6:4)

To whom, then, will you compare God?

What image will you compare him to?(Isaiah 40:18)

The God of the Bible is incomparable. Nothing can equal Him. He alone is the Supreme Being.

'I am the first and I am the Last;

apart from me there is no God'. (Isaiah 44:6)

"You shall have no other gods before me. You shall not make for yourself an idol in the form of anything ..." (Exodus 20:3-4) those are the first two commandments and they are first because there is no other god beside God. Nothing on this earth or in the universe can compare to Almighty God. We are not to worship the sun or the moon or the stars, animals, mankind, or the earth itself – not any created thing. An idol can be *anything,* or *anyone,* that replaces God in our affection; it is also any image (whether mental or physical), or a description of God that does not conform to what He has revealed of Himself in the Bible.

Idolatry is a major concern to God as is clear from the history of Israel. What caused the greatest harm to Israel was the turning away from true religion to false gods. There can be no compromise on this issue because God dearly wants us to know Him in perfect fellowship as He intended to be known. If we turn away from what He has revealed about Himself, then we will never know Him, nor will we ever experience His perfect love. **"Therefore, since we are God's offspring, we should not think that**

42

the divine being is like gold or silver or stone – an image made by man's design and skill. In the past God overlooked such ignorance, but now he commands all people everywhere to repent." (Acts 17:29-30)

Only the God of the Bible is worthy of worship, for there is only one God and one way to know Him. Jesus said, "I am the way and the truth and the life. No-one comes to the Father except through me." (John 14:6) "Now this is eternal life; that they may know you, the only true God, and Jesus Christ, whom you have sent." (John 17:3)

This is a controversial statement because it denies the belief that all religions are valid and it doesn't matter what you believe as long as you live a good life. 'All roads lead to God' is the view of today's culture. To say anything different brings upon us the accusation that we are bigots and inciting hatred. Well, it may be true that some people use religion for their own means, and do incite hatred, but the true Christian should never do that. We must demonstrate the love of God to everyone with total respect for human life, remembering that all people are made in the image of God. Asserting that there is one God and one way to Him does not mean that we are inciting people to hate those who believe differently from us.

It is important to note that the first Christians never attacked or ridiculed the belief of others. In the book of Acts, there is an account of a riot caused by tradesmen who sold idols. They were losing business because many in Ephesus were abandoning idols to worship Christ. Eventually, the city clerk quietened the angry crowd and said this about

Paul and the other Christians: **"You have brought these men here, though they have neither robbed temples nor blasphemed our goddess."** (Acts 19:37) Paul and the other believers preached Christ but never once attacked the beliefs of the Ephesians or smashed their idols; they let God do His work in people's hearts. We need to follow the example of these believers by asserting the truth in love, praying for everyone to know Jesus Christ and through Him, the one true God.

You may ask, 'Why are there so many religions in the world if there is only one God? Why should I believe that Jesus is the only way?' Religion and seeking to live in an upright, moral way are our efforts to reach God. The human heart knows that there is something more to life than the material world. Deep down, the imprint of God speaks. All human beings were made in His image, so then, that latent image – His imprint if you like – wants to reconnect with the Creator. But sin has distorted the image and blinded us to the truth. And we mustn't overlook the activity of the devil, who also deceives mankind into thinking we can reach God by our own efforts. Many religions contain some truth and good ethics, but that does not rescue us from the power of sin or Satan.

Biblical Christianity asserts that God has done what we fail to do. It is not about keeping rules, practising rituals, or living a moral life, but about trusting in what He has provided – His very own Son, who died in our place and rose from the dead never to die again. Later on, we will be looking in more detail at what Jesus achieved, but for now, let us grasp that the Bible claims that Jesus is unique and, as we will see in a moment, very God in human flesh. He is the only way to the Father because only He has conquered sin and evil. **For as in Adam all die, so in Christ all will be made alive.** (1 Corinthians 15:22)

God is a unity of three persons in one

If anything is beyond our understanding, it is the doctrine of the Trinity. Because our minds cannot grasp this amazing truth, many have rejected this teaching, backing up their view by saying that the word 'trinity' doesn't appear in the Bible, that it is a word created by theologians. That may be true, but the teaching that God is a unity of three Persons, who are distinct from each other but are one in essence, is in the Bible.

The Father is God. The Son is God. The Holy Spirit is God. They are distinct from each other, but they are all part of the one Supreme Being. This is a tri-unity – a unity of three in one. There are no illustrations that can fully help us understand the Trinity because nothing in this world compares to God, so I won't offer any as they always fall short and often cause more confusion. It is impossible for our minds to grasp how God can be one and yet three at the same time. This takes us back to the beginning, where we affirmed that God is beyond our understanding. Believing isn't about our ability to comprehend; it is about accepting what God has revealed. This teaching of the Trinity is implied in the Old Testament and fully revealed in the New.

The Trinity implied in the Old Testament

Three times in Genesis, God uses the plural when speaking of Himself. At Creation, we read: **In the beginning God created the heavens** (the sky) **and the earth... and the Spirit of God was hovering over the waters.** (Genesis 1:1, 2) **Then God said, "Let *us* make man in our image, in *our* likeness..."** (Genesis 1:26) After Adam sinned: **And the LORD God said, "The man has now become like one of *us*, knowing good and evil".** (Genesis 3:22) and at the tower of Babel: **"Come, let *us* go down and confuse their language..."** (Genesis 11:7)

Earlier, I spoke of the appearances of the Lord Jesus before He was born, and He is identified with the Angel of the LORD. That those who encountered the Angel of the LORD believed they had seen God is unmistakable. Take Moses' encounter with the Angel of the LORD: **There the Angel of the LORD appeared to him in flames of fire from within a bush ... When the LORD saw that he had gone over to look, God called to him from within the bush ... "Do not come any closer," God said. "Take off your sandals, for the place where you are standing is holy ground." Then he said, "I am the God of your father, the God of Abraham, the God of Isaac, and the God of Jacob." At this Moses hid his face, because he was afraid to look at God.** (Exodus 3:2, 4, 5, 6)

Then there's the, soon to be, parents of Samson **"... the Angel of the LORD ascended in the flame... "We are doomed to die!" he said to his wife, "We have seen God!""** (Judges 13) The clearest example of the Son appearing before He was born is found in Isaiah 6, where

Isaiah saw the Lord, who is described as "**Holy, holy, holy is the LORD Almighty...**" (Isaiah 6:3) We know that it was God the Son Isaiah saw because in the gospel of John, there is a quotation from Isaiah 6 and immediately afterwards John (guided by the Holy Spirit) states: "**Isaiah said this because he saw Jesus' glory and spoke about him.**" (John 12:41) These, and other references in the Old Testament, give hints of the Trinity, but it is in the New Testament that the Trinity is more explicit.

The Trinity revealed in the New Testament

The Trinity is seen in the message to Mary that she will bear a son: "**The Holy Spirit will come upon you, and the power of the Most High will overshadow you. So the holy one to be born will be called the Son of God.**" (Luke 1:35) In this verse, each Person of the Godhead is mentioned, the Holy Spirit, the Most High, and the Son of God.

All three persons of The Trinity are revealed in the baptism of Jesus. **As Jesus was coming up out of the water, he saw heaven being torn open and the Spirit descending on him like a dove. And a voice came from heaven; "You are my Son, whom I love; with you I am well pleased."** (Mark 1:10-11) Here we have the Son being baptised, the Spirit descending upon Him, and the Father speaking.

Jesus provides the clearest teaching of a unity of three in the Godhead. "**If you really knew me, you would know my Father as well. From now on, you do know him and have seen him... Anyone who has seen me has seen the Father... Don't you believe that I am in the Father, and**

that the Father is in me? The words I say to you are not just my own. Rather, it is the Father, living in me, who is doing his work. Believe me when I say that I am in the Father and the Father is in me; or at least believe on the evidence of the miracles themselves... And I will ask the Father, and he will give you another Counsellor to be with you forever – the Spirit of truth... the Counsellor, the Holy Spirit, whom the Father will send in my name, will teach you all things..." (Selected verses from John 14:7-26)

We see from the above verses Jesus identifying Himself with the Father and the Spirit, and it is hard to miss the point that they are one and the same. The works, or miracles, of Jesus, are evidence of His Divine nature, Jesus could not have done the things He did unless He had the Father's authority. We also see the different roles each person of the Godhead plays. The Father is the originator of creation and salvation. He sends the Son who became a man to reveal the Father to us and fulfil the Father's plan of salvation. The Son and the Father sends the Holy Spirit who makes both the Father and Son known to us, helping us to understand spiritual things and making us alive to God. **"But I will send you the Advocate—the Spirit of truth. He will come to you from the Father and will testify all about me."** (John 15:26 NLT) **"Unless I go away, the Counsellor will not come to you; but if I go, I will send him to you... But when he, the Spirit of truth, comes, he will guide you into all truth... He will bring glory to me by taking from what is mine and making it known to you.** (Selected verses from John 16: 7-14)

Two of the clearest declarations of the Deity of Christ are found in Romans 9 and Titus 2, where Paul is speaking about the legacy of the Jews. **"Theirs are the patriarchs, and from them is traced the human ancestry of Christ, who is *God over all*, forever praised! Amen."** (Romans 9:5) When Paul speaks of Christ's return: **...while we wait for the blessed hope– the appearing of the glory of our *great God* and Saviour, Jesus Christ...** (Titus 2:13b) It was Jesus' own claim to be God that caused Him to clash with the religious leaders of His day. He used the Divine name: **"I tell you the truth... before Abraham was born, I am!" At this, they picked up stones to stone him..."** (John 8:58-59) He claimed equality with God: **"I and the Father are one." Again the Jews took up stones to stone him. Jesus said to them, "I have shown you many great miracles from the Father. For which of these do you stone me?" "We are not stoning you for any to these," replied the Jews, "but for blasphemy, because you, being a mere man, claim to be God."** (John 10: 30-33) Jesus claimed to be God and it was for this claim that they sentenced Him to die. Those who deny the Deity of Christ are not listening to Him.

Jesus accepted worship as God: **Thomas said to him, "My Lord and my God!" Then Jesus told him, "Because you have seen me, you have believed; blessed are those who have not seen and yet have believed."** (John 20:28-29) Note that Jesus does not rebuke Thomas for calling Him God; instead, He confirms that those who believe will be blessed indeed. Jesus encourages His followers to think in terms of the Trinity: **"All authority in heaven and on earth has been given to me. Therefore go and make**

disciples of all nations, baptizing them in the name of the Father and of the Son and of the Holy Spirit... (Matthew 28:18-19) Here is a clear reference to a unity of three persons in one because He does not say in the names of, but the *name* – one single name but three distinct persons.

It is hardly surprising then that the teaching of the Trinity formed the basis for the message of the early Church. This is what Peter had to say on the day of Pentecost: **"God has raised this Jesus to life, and we are all witnesses of the fact. Exalted to the right hand of God, he has received from the Father the promised Holy Spirit and has poured out what you now see and hear."** (Acts 2:32) Of believers, Peter says: **"... who have been chosen according to the foreknowledge of God the Father, through the sanctifying work of the Spirit, for obedience to Jesus Christ..."** (1 Peter 1:2)

Paul talks about the gifts of the Spirit given by the same Spirit, the same Lord Jesus, and the same God. **"There are different kinds of gifts, but the same Spirit. There are different kinds of service, but the same Lord. There are different kinds of working, but the same God works all of them in all men."** (1 Corinthians 12:4-6)

There are many, many more passages of Scripture I could quote, but these are sufficient for us to understand that the doctrine of the Trinity wasn't an invention of the Church. It comes from the Bible and is the mark of authentic Biblical Christianity. For me, this is a proof of revealed religion because no created mind could have come up with a concept like this. It is a mind-boggling truth that makes the head hurt if we try to work it out. Those who deny that

God is a unity of three persons in one, do so because they want a god they can understand. Those with true faith will simply stand in awe and worship such a majestic Person.

<u>The Trinity helps us understand the nature of salvation</u>

Because God is a tri-unity He knows how to love, and He loves to save a fallen world. It is via the Trinity that God relates to us. He is the Father, a person and not a thing. We can have an intimate relationship with this Father. He loves us, gives us life, protects us, disciplines us, and provides for our every need. And He loved us so much He couldn't leave us wretched slaves to sin. He planned salvation.

The Son willingly carries out the plan of salvation, giving up His glory and humbling Himself to be born a helpless baby. The Son took on the name Jesus, meaning "saviour" or "God is Salvation." Jesus is the Greek translation of Joshua, and the 'J' would have been pronounced with a 'Y' sound, so Jesus was most probably called, Yeshua by His fellow Jews. Yeshua literary means, "Yahweh is Salvation", so His very name shows us that He is God. Matthew 1:23: "**...and they will call him Immanuel! – which means, "God with us."** Jesus is God with us – not God at a distance but God close-up. He shared our humanity with one major difference – He had no sin, nor did He sin, so He became the perfect sacrifice to turn away God's wrath from us sinners. We will be looking at this in more detail later on, but for now, if you want to know who the Father is, you need only to look at the Son. Someone described Him as God with a human face, not just an intangible Spirit, but someone like us.

The Father planned our salvation, the Son carried out the plan, providing the means of escape from the power of sin, and the Spirit applies that saving work to our lives. He convicts us of sin, making us aware of our need for salvation, bringing us to a point where we can turn away from sin and turn to the Son for mercy. The Holy Spirit makes our dead spirits alive to God, transforming us from slaves of sin to children of God. He carries out within us the work of restoring the image of God and making us like Jesus. The Spirit lives in the true believer's heart, helping them to understand the word of God. Jesus called Him the Helper, or Advocate, or Counsellor, all translations of a word meaning, 'to come alongside'. Think of a parent coming alongside a small child who is trying to write for the first time. The parent takes the little hand in theirs and gently guides it to form the letters. The Holy Spirit takes our hand and guides us. He helps us to resist temptation and to obey God's perfect will. He enables our spirits to connect to God the Father and God the Son, helping us understand what we need to know.

The doctrine of the Trinity is not a concept made up by theologians, it is who God is and He has revealed Himself so that we can know His wonderful love.

A Tri-unity of Love

Since writing the above, I have read an excellent book called, 'The Good God: Enjoying Father, Son, and Spirit' by Michael Reeves, which deals with this awesome doctrine in a clear, no-nonsense way that is like inhaling a refreshing sea breeze. I can't recommend the book highly enough.

Reeves' book helped me see that it is not enough just to say that we can't understand the Trinity because that leaves us with boggling minds and an impression of God which is cold and distant. I certainly don't want to do that. If I have made the Trinity sound all cold and technical then I apologise because the aim of my book, particularly this section, is to help us all appreciate what an awesome, amazing, beautiful, and loving Person God is.

At the heart of the Trinity is love. **God is love** (1 John 4:8). We readily accept that statement believing, quite correctly, that God loves us. But then we miss the truth that God is love because He is *Father, Son,* and *Spirit,* and each distinct person of this tri-unity loves the others. In other words, God is a unity of love. We get a wonderful glimpse of this loving relationship in the prayer of Jesus recorded in John 17. **"Father... you loved me before the creation of the world."** (John 17:24) So from before the creation, there has been and always will be, eternal love. If you read the whole of John 17, you can't miss how much Jesus loves His Father, and the Father loves the Son. What is more, this helps us to understand that God made us to be loved. He sent His Son to rescue us from sin not only because He loves us, but also so that we would experience the same love that He has for the Son. **"I have made you known to them, and will continue to make you known in order that the love you have for me may be in them and that I myself may be in them."** (John 17:26) Read that again – Jesus makes the Father known to us so that we experience the same love God has for the Son! In other words, God the Father accepts us as if we possessed the same pure, perfect goodness as Jesus! No longer treated as a wretched slave to sin, but as a deeply loved child of God – that's what a Christian is!

Chapter Three

The Eternal, Self-Existent, All Powerful God

God is Eternal

When I was an eleven-year-old schoolboy back in 1969, I remember the day the headmaster of my primary school came into our classroom to talk to us. The school had limited space, so assemblies of the whole school were rare, and we usually had what amounted to a little service, with a Bible story and prayer in our classroom led by our teacher. We were quite excited when the headmaster did the 'assembly' instead of our teacher.

I do not remember the name of that headmaster, but I will never forget the simple illustration he gave us that morning. He drew a circle on the blackboard and a straight line underneath it. The straight line represented our lives:

it had a beginning, middle, and an end, and so do we. We are born, we live and will eventually die. I remember not liking the bit about dying, but I became fascinated with the explanation of the circle. This represented God, just as a circle has no beginning, middle, or end, so God is eternal. No one made God, He wasn't born, and He will not die – He simply lives – He is.

Years later, when I was asked by a child, 'Who made God?', that simple illustration came back to mind, and I've used it ever since. Because we are locked in time, it is impossible for us to fully understand the idea of eternity, and once again, we try to grasp the wind when we attempt to fathom the nature of God. What we need is simple child-like acceptance. It made sense to me when I was a boy that God was eternal, if He could end, then He wouldn't be worth worshipping as God. God revealed His eternal nature when He told Moses what His name was: **"I AM WHO I AM. This is what you are to say to the Israelites: I AM has sent me to you." God also said to Moses, "Say this to the Israelites: Yahweh, the God of your fathers, the God of Abraham, the God of Isaac, and the God of Jacob, has sent me to you. This is My name forever; this is how I am to be remembered in every generation."** (Exodus 3:14-15 HCSB)

Because of the complexities of translating the name of God, there is no agreement as to what it really was and how it should be written. To avoid misusing God's name in obedience to the third commandment: **"Do not misuse the name of the Lord your God, because the Lord will not**

leave anyone unpunished who misuses His name." (Exodus 20:7 HCSB), Jews used a word, "ADONAI", meaning *my Lord* instead of saying the Sacred Name, that's why most English Bibles used the word, "LORD". The above translation shows two of God's names. I AM and Yahweh, both relate to a Hebrew verb, *to be*, so then, the personal name of God expresses eternity. He is the ever-present One. I AM WHO I AM, expresses the thought: 'I am who I have always been, I am who I am now, and I am what I will be in the future'. This thought is expressed when God addresses the Apostle John in Revelation. **"I am the Alpha** (the first letter of the Greek alphabet) **and the Omega,"** (the last letter of the Greek alphabet) **says the Lord God, "who is, and who was, and who is to come, the Almighty."** (Revelation 1:8)

The implications of God's eternal nature are immense. He is over and above time, transcending all history. He sees the beginning to the end of time. God is. God has always been, and God will always be. This is just wonderful! It means that even though we see change all around us, there is one who is constantly good at the heart of life. It also means that when we enter His presence, we will live with Him in eternity. Our lives may end on this earth but will continue forever, and that's because we possess an eternal soul. That's the benefit of being made in the image of the eternal God. As I stated in the introduction, we were created to live forever.

The other implication for true believers is that we have no real need to worry while we travel through this life on earth. We trust in a Person who knows all our past, our present, and our futures. Nothing takes God by surprise – nothing at all! Many people worry about the future (and I put my hand up as one of them), but it is pointless worrying when we trust in the Eternal One. Some people would like to know what their futures will unfold and go to fortune-tellers and mediums. This is pointless also because only God knows the future. Personally, I am glad that I don't know what's around the corner because if I knew that there was a hard time ahead, I would probably try to avoid it and never know if I could have overcome the difficulty with the Lord's help.

God has placed me in time and at this point in history. It is futile trying to live either in the past or the future; we need to trust Him in the present by living the life He has given us to the full, knowing with confidence that He knows our futures. On Christmas Day in 1939, King George the VI gave a speech to a country that had just entered the Second World War. He quoted from a poem written by Minnie Louise Haskins.

"And I said to the man who stood at the gate of the year: 'Give me a light that I may tread safely into the unknown.' And he replied: 'Go out into the darkness and put your hand into the Hand of God. That shall be to you better than light and safer than a known way.'"

God is self-existent and independent

Most young children have an imaginary friend at some stage in their development, but I had an imaginary car when I was about five or six. Wherever I went, I would "drive" this car. My mother, being the embodiment of patience, indulged my imagination when on our frequent walks to the shop. She would mimic opening the passenger door, pretend to step in the car, and close the door. She didn't walk until I said we could because I had to turn the "engine" on. What a picture I must have been happily pretending to turn an invisible steering wheel and imitating engine noises from the back of my throat, which didn't seem to bother my mother at all.

Sometimes my mother would forget to "open" the "door" before stepping out and received my reprimand graciously. She had an annoying habit of forgetting where we had parked, so there would be a little disagreement, and she would suggest that the car must have moved and I was mistaken, but I could *see* this car, and I *knew* where I'd parked it. Mum would eventually realise that I was right, and we would make our way back home, acting out the same pantomime. I looked forward to shopping trips, but I'm not sure if my mother did as she could do them in half the time without me as a chauffeur.

When I grew older, the car did an amazing thing: it vanished. As long as I believed in that car, it was very real to me, but as my imagination found other things to ponder, the car ceased to exist because I no longer believed in it. If I were to stop believing in God, He would do an amazing thing: He would *still* exist. My life would be impoverished by my lack of faith, but God would continue to be. The gods of Olympus needed the Greeks to believe in them, or they would fade away, and this is true of all pagan deities.

Atheists think they can do away with religion by turning society into a secular state with only self-belief to give life a purpose. But if you say that you don't believe in God, that does not affect God one little bit – it affects you. He does not depend on our faith in Him. He does not need you or me. He will never get lonely because the three Persons of the Trinity share perfect companionship. Children should not be encouraged to think that God made us because He was lonely; He made us because He wanted to. As we saw in the last chapter, He wanted to share the love He has for His Son with us! Without God, *we* would cease to exist. **'For in him we live and move and have our being.'** (Acts 17:28)

The thought that God does not need us is very sobering, and I have upset many people in the past whenever I stated this truth, but this is the teaching of the Bible. **"And he is not served by human hands, as if he needed anything, because he himself gives all men life and breath and everything else."** (Acts 17:25) Though God is independent of us, we are not independent of Him. Sin is the desire to rule our own lives without reference to God.

God can do anything without us, but amazingly, He chooses not to. The life lived with God is one of cooperation. We see this demonstrated in so many lives in the Bible from Noah, Abraham, Moses, Gideon, and Esther, right through to Peter and Paul. The people of the Bible were enriched when they cooperated with God and impoverished when they didn't. Because God desires us to share a personal relationship with Him, He is pleased to involve us in His work. I am often struck by the thought that this awesome Supreme Being, who holds the universe together, keeps every star in place, all the planets in their orbit, and engineers every tiny atom – the God who is All-Powerful, All-Knowing, Ever-Present, and Self-Existent – takes any notice of me and my prayers, but He does! He will listen to every heart that sincerely seeks Him. God wants to know us and for us to know Him, so He cooperates with us and invites us to pray. This Mighty God will do as we ask if we ask according to His will. Jesus said, **"I tell you the truth, my Father will give you whatever you ask in my name."** (John 16:23) Praying in the name of Jesus means that we are in tune with the Father and are praying according to His will.

Prayer keeps our first love alive, especially when expressed in a loving relationship with other believers. Corporate prayer is vital because it emphasises how we are part of a family called the body of Christ, cooperating with the head. God will act upon our prayers, especially when we are listening to Him and praying for what is on His heart. The Lord Jesus promised, **"Again I tell you that if two of you on earth agree about anything you ask for, it will be done for you by my Father in heaven. For where two or three come together in my name, there am I with them."** (Matthew 18:18-19)

The reference to agreeing is to do with Church discipline, forgiveness, and Church unity. We must have sincere transparent love for each other and not allow disagreements to tear us apart. God, who is love, listens to those who love one another. The prayer meeting isn't an optional extra to

Church life, it is the moment where the Mighty God who doesn't need us, because He is self-existing, chooses to work with us – that is how important prayer is.

God is All-Powerful

This is an obvious statement because the Person we've been looking at could be nothing less than all-powerful. We must never be tempted to reduce God to a mere intellectual exercise. A lot of people find the study of God interesting but put it alongside human philosophies. They can read the Bible and never engage with its author, missing the whole point of Bible study.

The God revealed in the Bible transcends any other concepts of deity to the conclusion that no one could have invented the God of the Bible. The human mind is too puny to be able to conceive a Person like this. God revealed His name to Abraham as **God Almighty.** (Genesis 17:1) He is more powerful than anything we can possibly imagine. **"For nothing is impossible with God."** (Luke 1:37)

".... with God all things are possible." (Matthew 19:26)

God's power is displayed in creation, not only in the fact that He made everything but also in the fact that He is ... **sustaining all things by his powerful word...** (Hebrews 1:3) His power keeps the universe together. He alone has perfect knowledge of it. You may say, 'Ah, but the scientists have explained much of our world, there are no mysteries anymore, and soon, they will have cracked the code of exactly how the universe formed.' Well, that may be the claim, but most of what science puts forward are theories, not facts. But this is not the place, and I am not the person to debate science versus faith. The fact is that there are still many things to discover about our world, and whatever science may find, the source of the power of creation is God. He is behind the great discoveries, and the things we achieve are made possible by His guidance alone.

Countless passages in the Bible describe God's power in terms of His sovereignty over the universe. In Job, Elihu anticipates what God later says of Himself when He says:

"Who appointed him over the earth?

Who put him in charge of the whole world?

**If it were his intention and he withdrew
his spirit and breath,**

**all flesh would perish together, and man
would return to dust."** (Job 34:13-15)

Elihu speaks of God's absolute right to rule the universe because He is the One who maintains it. If He were to remove His influence, then every person in the world would die. God does not go on holiday, nor does He nod off or sleep, He is constantly watching over His created realm. We can taste something of His Majesty in the following verses from Job and Isaiah.

"Where were you when I laid the earth's foundation?

Tell me, if you understand.

Who marked off its dimensions?

Surely you know!

Who stretched a measuring line across it?

On what were its footings set or who laid its corner-stone –

while the morning stars sang together

and all the angels shouted for joy?" (Job 38:4-7)

Do you not know?

Have you not heard?

Has it not been told you from the beginning?

Have you not understood since the earth was founded?

He sits enthroned above the circle of the earth,

and its peoples are like grasshoppers.

He stretches out the heavens like a canopy,

and spreads them out like a tent to live in.

He brings the princes to naught and

reduces rulers of this world to nothing...

"To whom will you compare me?

Or who is my equal?" says the Holy One.

(Isaiah 40:21-23)

I imagine God saying something like that to scientists who think they know it all. Of course, He speaks in poetic language, laced with irony. These verses show us that

God's power is over the peoples of the world, the nations, and all their rulers have to answer to the Almighty in the end. So, God's power speaks of His right to rule as well as His might. God has the right to do anything with us. He has the right to be worshipped. The right to be obeyed. The right to judge and decide our ultimate destiny. He is Sovereign – a Mighty King who rules the universe He made and sustains.

Chapter Four

The All-Knowing, All-Present, Transcendent One

God is All Knowing

Nothing takes God by surprise. All history is in His hands as He knows the beginning to the end. His knowledge is complete because He knows everything. The logical conclusion is that God does not need to learn as we do – He is the One who imparts wisdom to men. It is safe to say that the Lord Jesus was the greatest teacher in all history. He will never be surpassed, even by the most accomplished thinkers and scientists, because He possessed the knowledge of His Father – His teaching is directly from the Father – it is God's wisdom that Jesus displays.

God's knowledge of us is also complete, something that the psalmist delighted in.

O LORD, you have searched me and know me.

You know when I sit and when I rise; you perceive my thoughts from afar.

You discern my going out and my lying down; you are familiar with all my ways.

Before a word is on my tongue, you know it completely O LORD. (Psalm 139:1-4) The fact that God knows my thoughts before I think them and my words before I speak them makes me pray:

Set a guard over my mouth, O LORD;

keep watch over the door of my lips. (Psalm 141:3)

The idea of a person who knows absolutely everything about me is frightening. Sometimes I feel that we have lost the sense of awe in worship. We can be too familiar with God and forget His perfect knowledge of us. We are sinners approaching a Holy God, and so we need a holy fear of this God. Talking about the fear of God is not popular, and often it is watered down to merely respecting God. It does mean to respect, but it also means what it says. If I fear God, I will be afraid to offend Him and will change my way of life. **Be not wise in your own eyes; fear the LORD and turn away from evil.** (Proverbs 3:7 ESVUK)

When I fear God, I admit that He has the right to judge me, and I will wholeheartedly desire to please Him. But this fear is not a base, cringing, irrational fear, as displayed by a neurotic; this fear of God is an aspect of our love for Him. When we genuinely love God, we fear to grieve Him in any way. We will desire to please Him and keep away from anything that would offend the One we love.

A benefit of fearing God is that we will not be afraid of anything else. Are you worried about the past, present, or future? Jesus said: **"Do not be afraid. I am the First and the Last."** (Revelation 1:17) **"So don't worry about tomorrow, for tomorrow will bring its own worries. Today's trouble is enough for today."** (Matthew 6: 34 NLT) Do you worry about what someone thinks or says about you? **The LORD is for me, so I will have no fear. What can mere people do to me?** (Psalm 118:6 NLT) Are you worried about food, clothing, housing, or your job or lack of work? **"So do not worry, saying, 'What shall we eat?' or 'What shall we drink?' or 'What shall we wear?' For... your heavenly Father knows that you need them."** (Matthew 6:31-32) Are you a person who frets about the unknown or the supernatural? **The reason the Son of God appeared was to destroy the devil's work.** (1 John 3:8)

Are you afraid to share your faith? Do you fear persecution from workmates, family, or friends? No one likes being rejected, and when we share our Christian convictions with others, we risk being mocked and excluded. Jesus warned His disciples that persecution would come and commanded them to proclaim His message, fearing only God the Father. **"Do not be afraid of those who kill the body but cannot kill the soul. Rather, be afraid of the**

One who can destroy both soul and body in hell." (Matthew 10:28) When I first read that passage, before I was a Christian, I mistakenly thought the Lord meant the devil. But He means God the Father who will hurl Satan into hell and all evil with him, so then, I need to fear God and shun evil.

There was an expression used a lot when I was a child: 'I'll put the fear of God in you'. The idea was that you would avoid doing wrong because you were afraid of God's punishment. I went through a phase when I was eleven of swearing a lot, but that got me into trouble with my parents, so I tried to stop, and in my childish way, I made a promise to God that I would not swear. I was so terrified that He would punish me if I did; I stopped swearing – for a while anyway. Avoiding punishment is a negative reason for fearing God.

However, there is a positive reason for fearing this Holy Person; we do so out of love and knowing that He, who knows and loves us completely, is good and will also protect us from evil. He has perfect knowledge of what goes on in His world. Jesus went on to say: **"Are not two sparrows sold for a penny? Yet not one of them will fall to the ground apart from the will of your Father. And even the very hairs of your head are all numbered. So don't be afraid; you are worth more than many sparrows."** (Matthew 10:29-31) When we are in love; it is fear of hurting the beloved that keeps us focused on pleasing them. If we genuinely love God, we will not want to offend Him or hurt Him in any way.

Whatever is happening in the world, no matter what circumstances we find ourselves in, no matter how great the suffering, the child of God can be confident of safety in our Father's loving hands and ultimate victory over adversity, pain, and death. Your future is in God's hand, He knows all things, He knows you intimately, loves you totally, so you need not be afraid of anything else.

God is All-Present

Being Spirit means that God is limitless and not confined by a physical body, and just as air covers the entire world at once, so God is not confined to one place or one time.

Where can I go from your Spirit?

Where can I flee from your presence?

If I go up to the heavens, you are there;
if I make my bed in the depths, you are there.

If I rise on the wings of the dawn, if I settle on
the far side of the sea,

even there your hand will guide me, your
right hand will hold me fast.

If I say, "Surely the darkness will hide me
and the light become night

around me", even the darkness will not
be dark to you;

the night will shine like the day, for
darkness is as light to you. (Psalm 139:7-11)

King David's beautiful poem portrays a high view of God, so different from the pagan world around him. The gods of the pagans were territorial and limited to one place. There were gods of the sky, hills, valleys, seas, rain, in fact a multitude of territorial gods. The Greeks of Paul's day worshipped Zeus, the king of the gods of Olympus. He was the god of the sky, wielding a lightning bolt. Apollo looked after the sun, Poseidon, the sea, Hades, the realm of the dead, Pan looked after nature, and on and on it goes with lesser gods in charge of different territories. In Homer's Iliad, Zeus relies on Iris, the messenger goddess, for information. Zeus can be defeated, he gets tired, he needs to sleep, so there is no way he can be everywhere. This idea of many limited gods, each in charge of their own territory, was common to all pagan religions, especially the gods of the nations who lived around Israel. What a contrast the LORD is! ... **indeed, he who watches over Israel will neither slumber nor sleep.** (Psalm 121: 4) Psalm 139:8 says that **"if I should go to the depths, the LORD is there."** The "depths" is a translation of a Hebrew word meaning the places under the earth, or more commonly, the place of the dead, so the LORD rules over all things, including the afterlife.

In the book of Kings, there is an incident where Israel's enemies made the mistake of thinking that Yahweh was the same as their gods. They launched a plan to attack Israel in the valleys rather than the mountains, **"Then the man of God approached and said to the king of Israel, "This is what the LORD says: 'Because the Arameans have said: Yahweh is a god of the mountains and not a god of the valleys, I will hand over all this great army to you. Then you will know that**

I am the LORD.'" (1 Kings 20:28 HCSB) The Arameans got a bloody nose that day and learned the hard way that Yahweh God was not just the God of Israel but of all the earth, and He is not confined to one territory.

Jonah was a disobedient prophet. He ran away – literally in the other direction from the one God had ordered him to go. Of course, Jonah found that trying to get away from God was impossible. Calamity came upon the crew of the ship he was on. The pagan crew drew lots to see who had offended the god of the sea and caused the fierce storm, and Jonah drew the short straw. He explains that he is running away from God, **"I am a Hebrew. I worship Yahweh, the God of the heavens, who made the sea and the dry land. Then the men were even more afraid..."** (Jonah 1:9, 10 HCSB) The crew were terrified because Jonah's God wasn't limited to one place, unlike their deities: He is the God of all the earth. Every nation is answerable to God. Even those who do not acknowledge His existence are dependent upon Him for life, for He provides the seasons, the food, and everything we need. The Bible speaks of a day when all nations will be judged by this Holy Being.

The comfort for believers in knowing that God is all-present is immense. He is with every believer. He is accessible to all who trust in Him, and there is absolutely no place we can be separated from Him. When you are in that dark place of difficulty and suffering, remember even the darkness is not dark to God. You may not feel God's presence, all seems hopeless and confusing, but He is with you, right there holding on to you. Wherever you go, He is there, and there is nothing in this universe, either physical or spiritual, that can separate the child of God from their Father in Heaven.

For I am convinced that neither death nor life, neither angels nor demons, neither the present nor the future, nor any powers, neither height nor depth, nor anything else in all creation, will be able to separate us from the love of God that is in Christ Jesus our Lord. (Romans 8: 38-39)

God is Transcendent

God is beyond the created universe. He is outside of time and space. This fact is implied in calling God Holy; while the primary meaning of the word means to be absolutely good, the word holy also means separate, or to set apart, and so can be applied to His transcending the universe.

God is set apart from creation; He is not dependent on it, nor is He to be confused with it. Pantheism is the belief that God is in every created thing and everything is sacred. Trees, mountains, seas, rivers, and animals are all part of God. The superstition of 'touching wood' to ward off bad luck has its roots in pantheism because the pagans would touch wood to venerate the tree spirit. The popular fantasy films "Star Wars" and "Avatar" contain pantheistic beliefs. The planet in the latter is "alive", it even thinks and defends itself while being controlled by a living tree. In the former series of films, certain enlightened people can tap into the "Force" which is an energy field inhabiting the universe and living in all things.

These beliefs have their origins in pagan religions, and paganism is thriving in the West, or so we are led to believe by the media. Adherents to the "New Age" religion are pantheistic when they talk of "Mother Earth" – a deity in their eyes. Pagan religions in other parts of the world are held up as examples to those in more "civilised" cultures. Some years ago, the media reported on an obscure tribe in South America who came out of isolation to rebuke those of us in the West, 'You are hurting our mother,' was their message.

Environmentalists seize upon this idea and saving the planet has become a major "new" religion. It is also big business with recycling and "environmentally friendly" products. Ordinary folk have pressure put upon them to recycle rubbish, conserve energy, cut down fuel emissions, save water, and so on. Rumours of fines for those who refuse come and go, but there's no doubt that many environmentalists have a zeal that is evangelistic and frightening in its intensity.

Now, don't misunderstand me, I myself recycle rubbish and try to care for the environment. It is only right and proper to do so. What I am objecting to is making the Earth and the rest of the universe into a god – the universe is not a god – nor is the God of the Bible part of the universe. God is a Person, not an energy force. Neither is He in a tree, a rock, or anything else – He is bigger than the universe and everything in it. By taking on board these pantheistic ideas, we are doing what the ancients did: **They exchanged the truth of God for a lie and worshiped and**

served created things rather than the Creator – who is forever praised. (Romans 1:25)

God gave Mankind the authority to rule the world and care for it. We are stewards of God's wonderful creation, and it is only right that His people behave responsibly towards the environment. The law given to Moses taught the Jews to care for the land and not to abuse animals. Every seventh year the land was not to be farmed but allowed to rest and lie fallow. **"For six years sow your fields, and for six years prune your vineyards and gather their crops. But in the seventh year the land is to have a sabbath of rest, a sabbath to the LORD. Do not reap what grows of itself or harvest the grapes of your untended vines. The land is to have a year of rest."** (Leviticus 25:3-5) It is a disgrace that we pollute the planet and litter the streets. Our greed has led to intensive farming of land and sea to the detriment of both; we need to farm according to Biblical principles, which help us care for the environment.

Respect for creation is good, we enjoy it more, but we do so not to the extent of worshipping it. No, we must worship God who transcends creation and is greater than any pagan invention of deity. As we have already stated, He is beyond our understanding, and transcends all human thought and philosophy.

Chapter Five

The Holy, Just and

Merciful One

God is Holy

What made Israel stand out from all the other nations around them was their concept of One Almighty, Holy God. Pagan gods were reflections of sinful humanity – supermen and superwomen – with the sin of humanity magnified to super proportions. Pagan worship demanded human sacrifice, temple prostitution, and orgies to ensure a harvest. The Israelites, when keeping the Law of Moses, rejected all those practices. They worshipped an invisible God, who is different from all other concepts of greatness and deity. He didn't need to be coaxed into providing for them, and He demanded holiness of His people. They were to be separate from the other nations and all the immoral practises associated with pagan worship. When Israel was holy, the nation was great. They brought civilisation to the world – or more accurately – their God brought about a great civilisation that was a light to the world. Under the kings, David and Solomon, Israel flourished as a great ancient power because at its heart was the worship of Yahweh – the One True Holy God. It was whenever they forsook God that Israel became impoverished.

Holiness is the distinguishing quality of God the Father, Son and Spirit. Each Person of the Godhead is described in the Bible as being Holy. **"Holy Father..."** (John17:11) **"...your holy servant Jesus..."** (Acts 4:27) and of course, the **"Holy Spirit..."** (Acts 4:31)

> **"Holy, holy, holy is the Lord God Almighty,**
>
> **who was, and is, and is to come!"** (Revelation 4:8)

As we have seen, the word holy means to be set apart and separate. The primary meaning is to be set apart from sin and all that is evil. To describe God as Holy, we mean that He is morally perfect. He is completely good without any blemish at all. **God is light; in him there is no darkness at all.** (1John 1:5) The corrupt human mind could never have conceived the Holy One because we struggle to comprehend absolute purity. **Your eyes are too pure to look on evil; you cannot tolerate wrong.** (Habakkuk 1:13) God is a perfect Being, incapable of doing wrong, or evil of any kind, which is totally against His nature. There is no dark side to God. His moral purity is constant. Sin is the rejection of God and His goodness. Evil is to do what God hates and to go against this perfect Person.

Someone once said to me that to say that God is good and the Lord Jesus is perfect, is to make God a cold, unfeeling, distant Being. But I don't agree with that because His Holiness is not separate from His love. I see goodness as something warm, wonderful, kind, and compassionate, whereas evil is cold, calculating, and cruel. God is good! He is a Person you can trust to do what is right all the time. However, I can understand why the human heart would shrink from the idea of God being perfect, because His holiness presents us with a huge problem...

Good is opposed to evil – completely opposed – so different that they cannot co-exist. Light cancels out the dark. That is a remarkably simple fact: you turn on a light in a dark room, and the darkness vanishes. Light is used frequently in the Bible as a symbol of God's utter goodness, for just as light banishes the dark, so Good banishes evil. For us, who have corrupt natures and sin, it means we are banished from God, which results in spiritual death. The sinful person cannot view God as a loving Father but only as a judge against their sins. The Holiness of God results in His justice.

God is Just

God is Just, meaning He is fair and impartial. Another word to describe this attribute is righteousness – God is righteous – He will always do what is right and morally perfect. If He did not judge evil, He would be denying His very nature – He would stop being Good.

Because He is completely good; He must remove sin from His presence. He must deal with evil and remove it from His creation. I have just described the word Hell – Hell is complete eternal separation from God. Hell is another unpopular idea today, but we can't ignore it because our Lord Jesus warned against Hell many times, indeed it is from His lips that the most fearsome images of Hell are to be found. Hell is where God's wrath is poured out upon sin and evil, it is not to know the love of God but only the justice, righteousness, and complete holiness of God. The law that God gave to Moses is an expression of His justice. If we keep the law, we live. When we break the law, we die. That's justice; it is getting what we deserve. The purpose of the law is threefold:

1. <u>The law reveals the character of God</u>. The Ten Commandments recorded in Exodus 20:1-17 and Deuteronomy 5:6-21 show us that there is only one unique God. He is Spirit, so we are not to make idols. He is Holy, so we honour His name, set a day aside to worship Him and get to know Him. We see His love and provision in giving us parents and how parents point to the Fatherhood of God. We learn of His attitude to sin and how we reflect His love to one another in the remaining five commands not to murder, commit adultery, steal, lie and covet.

2. <u>The law reveals our need for God</u>. The law holds up a mirror to our sinful natures. From the law, we learn what sin is and how we can't be free from it by our own efforts. Paul makes this very clear in Romans 7:7 "... **I would not have known what sin was except through the law. For I would not have known what coveting really was if the law had not said, "Do not covet."** There I was, wanting things instead of God, desiring the stuff others had, getting

immersed in consumerism to the extent that I forgot about God and didn't know that was wrong. Until that is, I read the law. Then I not only knew I was sinful but knew I couldn't stop myself from sinning and needed God to help me.

3. <u>The law demonstrates our love for God</u>. By doing what God wants, we show that we love Him, and indeed, love should be the motive for obeying the law of God. We must never keep the law as a means of getting what we want. The comedian, Tony Hancock, was popular in the 1950s and 60s. In one of his programmes, "The Blood Donor", he produces a little book with all the good deeds he has done to date, which do not amount to very much. He states that when he dies, he'll show God the little book, and that would prove that he was worthy to enter Heaven. Of course, Tony Hancock was being humorous, but he exposed a tendency within us all to try and bribe our way into God's favour. The law cannot be used this way; we can only keep it when we love the One who gave it.

"If you love me, you will obey what I command." (John 14:15) **"Whoever has my commands and obeys them, he is the one who loves me."** (John 14:21) **"... 'Hear, O Israel, the Lord our God, the Lord is one. Love the Lord your God with all your heart and with all your soul and with all your mind and with all your strength.' The second** (greatest command) **is this: 'Love your neighbour as yourself.' There is no commandment greater than these."** Mark 12:29-31). But in case you think I'm saying anyone can keep the law of God, then think again. The standards of God are absolute perfection,

81

so it is impossible to be saved from sin by keeping the Law of Moses.

<u>The seriousness of sin</u>

"There is nothing more fatal than a failure to realize the terrible power of sin. Sin is the greatest power next to God Himself. It is so powerful that even God's Holy Law cannot deliver us." (Martyn Lloyd-Jones) We need to understand how awful, how deadly sin is. I have met many people who claim to be without sin. They say, 'I'm not a sinner!' What they usually mean is that they don't do certain things, like murder, robbing a bank, or rioting. They have limited sin to a few examples, and if they don't do those things, they are not sinners in their own eyes. However, these same people will think nothing of gossiping and spreading false rumours about others in violation of the ninth commandment. They will think nothing of taking something they consider small, like a pencil, from work in violation of the eighth commandment. They think nothing of having statues of Buddha in their homes or other religious icons in violation of the second commandment. I could go on, but I think I've made my point.

The truth is: **There is no difference, for all have sinned and fall short of the glory of God...** (Romans 3:23) That means we are all guilty of sin, and everyone has been born with a sinful nature, which eventually drags us into disobeying God. You and I are sinners – we may not like that, but that is the truth. **If we claim to be without sin, we deceive ourselves, and the truth is not in us.** (1 John 1:8)

It was when I read the Bible for the first time that I was confronted with my own sinfulness. I had a good moral upbringing, I wasn't a rebellious teenager, I respected my parents. I led a quiet, shy existence, worked hard, didn't smoke, drink, or have sex outside of marriage. Because I didn't do these things, I thought I was a good Christian. Then I read Jesus' teaching in the Sermon on the Mount in Matthew's Gospel, **"You have heard it was said, 'Do not commit adultery.' But I tell you that anyone who looks at a woman lustfully has already committed adultery with her in his heart."** (Matthew 5: 27-28) and I discovered that I was neither good nor a Christian because God is offended by thoughts and desires as much as actions.

Jesus aimed His message at all who are self-righteous (as I was) and think they are not sinners. The essence of His teaching is that it is not enough to keep the letter of the law while ignoring the heart and spirit of the law. For example, you may not have literally murdered someone but be honest, is there a person in your life who gets on your nerves, or you can't stand, even hate? Have you cursed them in your heart and wished harm upon them? Do you gossip? Have you spread rumours? Have you assassinated their character? **"You have heard that it was said to our ancestors, Do not murder, and whoever murders will be subject to judgement. But I tell you, everyone who is angry with his brother will be subject to judgement. And whoever says to his brother, 'Fool!' will be subject to the Sanhedrin.** (The Jewish ruling council, like a law court) **But whoever says, 'You moron!' will be subject to hellfire."** (Matthew 5:21- 22 HCSB). Hate is the seed of murder.

Outwardly, you may be living a very moral life. You may not be engaging in sex outside marriage or have never slept with anyone other than your spouse. But how do you look at the opposite sex? Have you let your gaze linger on an attractive person? How's that friendship going with a work colleague, all as it should be, or do you engage in "harmless" flirting? Whether you're married or single, are you careful about what you watch and what you read? Do you avoid sexually explicit or even just suggestive images? **"You have heard it was said, 'Do not commit adultery.' But I tell you that anyone who looks at a woman lustfully has already committed adultery with her in his heart."** (Matthew 5: 27-28)

When we dwell upon sinful desires, they eventually give birth to sinful deeds. Jesus stressed that it is what is in the heart that matters most. **"For from within, out of people's hearts, come evil thoughts, sexual immoralities, thefts, murders, adulteries, greed, evil actions, deceit, lewdness, stinginess, blasphemy, pride and foolishness. All these evil things come from within and defile a person."** (Mark 7:21-23 HCSB)

We can all underestimate the power of sin. I'm not a gardener, I even think that some weeds look pretty. I once praised some attractive white flowers growing on a bush, only to be told that they were the product of vine-weed. When I looked closer, I could see that the bush was practically dead, having been strangled by a wiry vine. When I attempted to remove the weed, I made matters worse. It was everywhere, and it had tangled itself around the bush so completely, that the bush was a brown shrivelled mess.

That is what sin is like. It looks attractive, even harmless, but it is insidious, deadly and it will choke the life out of your soul. It is impossible to remove it ourselves because we are so entangled.

We must grasp the enormity of sin, its eternal consequences, if we are to understand God's justice. He is Just so then; He will be decisive against this killer and see an end to it because He loves His creation – He loves you and me so much He will not let sin keep us as prisoners. God being Just, means that He hates sin. Sin is rebellion against this Holy God. Sin makes God angry and He acts against it.

Those who deliberately rebel against this Holy God demonstrate that they hate Him and will never enter His presence, instead, they will face the consequences of their deeds. **The wrath of God is being revealed from heaven against all the godlessness and wickedness of men who suppress the truth by their wickedness, since what may be known about God is plain to them, because God has made it plain to them.** (Romans 1:18-19) **For the wages of sin is death, but the gift of God is eternal life in Christ Jesus our Lord.** (Romans 6:23) Sin brings death and eternal separation from God, but God is not only Just, He is also full of love and mercy and so gives us the gift of eternal life in Christ Jesus.

God is Merciful

Mercy is love demonstrated to someone by forgiveness. Whereas justice is getting what we deserve, mercy is getting what we don't deserve. God's standards are absolute perfection so there is no way we, who are imperfect, can keep His law. There is nothing we can do to earn His forgiveness.

God is love. That is a statement and attribute of God we can readily accept. The three Persons of the Trinity share perfect love for all eternity, so God did not create us or the universe because He was lonely. He created us because love expresses itself in giving life. God made us because *He wanted to.* He is love; He wants us to know and enjoy His love. His love causes Him to show mercy to sinners instead of wrath. Psalm 103 is a prayer of King David, where he reminds himself that God loves him. It describes God's love expressed through mercy in far better words than I can think of:

The LORD is merciful and gracious,

slow to anger and abounding in steadfast love.

He will not always chide,

nor will he keep his anger forever.

He does not deal with us according to our sins,

nor repay us according to our iniquities.

For as high as the heavens are above the earth,

so great is his steadfast love towards those who fear

him;

as far as the east is from the west,

so far does he remove our transgressions from us.

As a father shows compassion to his children,

so the LORD shows compassion to those who fear

him. (Psalm 103:8-13, ESVUK)

Mercy is at the heart of this statement: **"As surely as I live," declares the Sovereign LORD, "I take no pleasure in the death of the wicked, but rather that they turn from their ways and live. Turn! Turn from your evil ways! Why will you die, O house of Israel?"** (Ezekiel 33: 11) This is the LORD God pleading with rebellious Israel to turn back to Him because He longs to show them His mercy and not His wrath. He does not enjoy punishing us and takes no pleasure in the death of the wicked.

God is patient, and His nature is to pour out mercy upon us: **The Lord is merciful and gracious, slow to anger and abounding in steadfast love.** (Psalms 103:8 ESVUK) However, God cannot simply forgive sin and ignore His justice because He must deal with evil, and if we do not teach about judgement and overemphasise His love, we misrepresent Him. Martyn Lloyd-Jones said, 'If God forgave sin without ministering His own justice, He would no longer be God.' This is because God is both Just and merciful, which presents us with a paradox.

A paradox is when two things that are true but completely different, indeed, opposite to each other, come together in the same thing. It is a statement that seems impossible because of two opposing ideas being true. God is Just: He must punish sin to be true to His Just and Holy

87

nature. God is love: He must show mercy to be true to His loving nature. If we were to ask a human judge to condemn a criminal and set him free at the same time, the judge would resign in dismay. But the God of Heaven found a way of being both just and merciful, and this forms the heart of the Bible's message, which we will look at in the next chapter.

Chapter Six

Justice and Mercy meet

at the Cross

When I saw the film, "The Passion of the Christ", I found it disturbing. The film starts with Jesus praying in the Garden of Gethsemane. When He is arrested, He is given a vicious blow around the head, causing blood to spatter out. As He is being led to the High Priest, He is suddenly pushed off a ridge and dangled from a great height. The violence against Jesus increases in graphic detail, and the depiction of the beating and crucifixion is sickening – it makes you want to turn away.

The director, Mel Gibson, obviously wanted to show the reality of the cross because, to us, the cross is a picture in a stained-glass window or piece of shiny jewellery. Many have no idea how offensive the symbol of the cross can be. It was the Roman equivalent to the gallows or the electric chair but designed so that the victim would suffer shame, humiliation, and slow, agonising death.

Crucifixion was so horrendous that the Romans never crucified their own citizens; they reserved it for their slaves and enemies. Before the victim was hung on a cross, they were sentenced to be scourged. A scourge was a whip of many strands with bits of metal and bone fastened to it. One lash was enough to tear the skin off a person's back. Many died of scourging alone. When Jesus was beaten in this way, the Roman soldiers vented all their hatred for the Jews and added mocking to the torment. Large thorns were pressed onto His head to mimic a crown, and the soldiers spat in His face.

Mel Gibson was right in showing that the victim was scarred beyond recognition, and he may have had the reference from Isaiah in mind to show how that prophecy was fulfilled in Jesus:

Just as there were many who were appalled at him –

his appearance was so disfigured

beyond that of any man and his form marred beyond human likeness... (Isaiah 52:14)

After the scourging, the condemned man was made to carry the crossbeam through the streets to the place of execution. There they would be stripped of all clothes and all remaining dignity. Nails were driven through the wrists, and the ankles, and the person was made to sit on a little bar to support their body, and this resulted in a slow agonising death caused by suffocation. The heart would eventually break from the strain.

The physical sufferings of Christ were indeed very great, but in concentrating on the gore, we ignore the spiritual sufferings of Christ. The Bible doesn't describe the actual crucifixion; there are no graphic details of the beating. There are no details of the nails in the flesh, the Gospel writers simply state that He was crucified. There was no need to describe it because the first readers of the Bible were familiar with Roman crucifixion.

Although the Bible was written not just for those first-century believers but for us today, the Holy Spirit directed the writers not to concentrate upon the physical agony but on the spiritual sufferings. They are more concerned with the *reason why* Jesus died, which is why the account of His sufferings begins on the night before He was hung on the cross.

He bore God's wrath

They went to a place called Gethsemane, and Jesus said to his disciples, "Sit here while I pray." He took Peter, James and John along with him, and he began to be deeply distressed and troubled. (Mark 14:32-33) Troubled and deeply distressed are powerful words conveying an intense inner struggle with fierce spiritual and emotional pain. The Amplified Bible translates these words as **He began to be struck with terror and amazement and deeply troubled and depressed.** (Mark 14:33 Amplified Bible) Jesus' own words have tremendous emotional power and

91

show a man in spiritual torment. **"My soul is over-whelmed with sorrow to the point of death."** (Mark 14:34) Again let's see what the Amplified Bible says: **My soul is exceedingly sad (overwhelmed with grief) so that it almost kills Me!** (Mark 14:34 Amplified Bible)

This is the same man who was determined to go to Jerusalem, knowing that death awaited Him there. **As the time approached for him to be taken up to heaven, Jesus resolutely set out for Jerusalem.** (Luke 9:51) This is the man who repeatedly warned His disciples that in Jerusalem, He would be killed. He knew and warned His disciples that He was going to die and did nothing to prevent it. So why was Jesus tormented in the garden? Was He suddenly afraid of dying and tempted to run away? I don't think so, there was undoubtedly testing going on, but I don't believe it was fear that was overwhelming Him. To understand what is happening, we need to pay attention to what Jesus says because He tells us what is happening. "My soul is exceedingly *sorrowful.*" He is overwhelmed with sorrow to the point that the pain of grief almost killed Him. His very essence, His soul, His person, is drowning in sorrow! It was a deep depression and extreme sadness that Jesus was experiencing.

The nature of His torment, causing him so much sorrow, was what would happen within the Godhead. Something of eternal, cosmic significance was about to occur between Father, Son and Spirit. Jesus urges His disciples; **"Stay here and keep watch." Going a little further, he fell to the ground and prayed that, if possible, the hour might pass from him. "Abba, Father," he said, "everything is**

possible for you, take this cup from me." (Mark 14:34-36) To us, these are very strange words, and to understand what the Lord meant by referring to a cup, we need to know what the Old Testament has to say because He is using imagery taken from the prophets. **"Rise up O Jerusalem, you who have drunk from the hand of the LORD the cup of his wrath..."** (Isaiah 51:17)

"Take from my hand this cup filled with the wine of my wrath and make all the nations to whom I send you drink it. When they drink it, they will stagger and go mad because of the sword I will send among them." (Jeremiah 25:15)

"You will be filled with drunkenness and sorrow,

the cup of ruin and desolation..." (Ezekiel 23:33)

Jesus is referring to imagery of God's wrath as a cup of bloody red wine poured out on the ground. This cup is the symbol of God's righteous judgement upon sin. Atheists are wrong when they say that the God of the Bible is an angry, cruel, and vengeful God who takes a sadistic enjoyment in the torment of the wicked. As we have already seen, God takes no delight in the death of the wicked. Those who dwell upon God's love and totally ignore His wrath are also wrong. We must grasp the fact that God's wrath is not like our anger in any way.

When we get angry, it is often personal, selfish, and petty. God's anger, in contrast, is the *proper response to sin*. It is a righteous anger, a deep, steady, controlled response to evil that has harmed His creation, including us. It is anger directed at evil in order to remove it. His wrath towards sin is consistent with His love. It is *because* He loves us He deals with sin. It is at the cross that justice and mercy meet.

There was an agreement within the Trinity before creation – before time began – that God the Son would take on human flesh and bear the sins of the world. **In the beginning was the Word...** A word is a means of communication, a way of expressing our thoughts and feelings to reveal what is in our hearts. Giving Jesus the title, the Word, the Bible tells us that the Son is God's communication to us and His way of revealing Himself, of making Himself known. The Word is eternal, **and the Word was with God...** He was, and is, a distinct person in the Godhead, **and the Word was God.** (John 1:1) He is, in very nature, God.

The Word became flesh and made his dwelling among us. (John 1:14) God the Son became a human being – not merely by taking on the shape of a man but by being born a helpless baby and sharing our humanity. He gave up the glory of Heaven for a stable and a cross. Jesus was conceived and born without sin, and throughout His life on earth, He never sinned. Just as some deny the Deity of Christ, so some deny His humanity. But we must be clear that the Bible teaches that Jesus was fully human and fully God. He is not half man and half God but *all* man and *all* God. He is the God-Man. This is another paradox we cannot understand but must accept by faith.

Incidentally, there is a danger of becoming too familiar with Jesus and forgetting that He is God and king, so we need to give Him His full title now and again as a mark of respect and not simply refer to Him as Jesus. He is the Lord Jesus Christ. Earlier, we saw that one of the names of God was Adonai, translated as 'Lord' in our Bibles. LORD is a translation of the name Yahweh. When we see LORD, we know that it refers to God the Father, and Lord means God the Son.

Why is it important that we grasp that Jesus is fully God and fully human? It is important because it is how God can be just and merciful. Being both God and man, the Lord Jesus became the supreme go-between. He represents God to us and us to God. As God, He breaks down the barrier of sin, letting us know the Father. As man, He becomes the ultimate substitute, dying in our place. The perfect, sinless man would have the wrath of the Father poured out upon Him, and it is *this* prospect that causes Jesus' heart to be torn with sorrow in the Garden of Gethsemane.

Jesus was about to be abandoned by His Father. The Father who declared of Jesus, **"You are my Son, whom I love; with you I am well pleased."** (Mark 1:11), was about to turn His face away from Him. The eternal fellowship between the Father and the Son was to be broken. Jesus meant every word when He cried out in the darkness, hanging from that tree, **"My God, my God, why have you forsaken me?"** (Mark 15:34) He *was* forsaken, abandoned, and rejected. I have always marvelled at the phrase: "God was forsaken of God." It wasn't a mere feeling of being forsaken – it was a dreadful reality.

Here, in the garden, He begins to feel the hand of wrath upon Him as His soul drowns in sorrow. His prayer is saying something like this: 'Is there another way? If there is another way, take this cup from Me, but only if there is another way – not what I want – but what You want!' The name Gethsemane means olive press. In this garden, they must have squeezed the pure oil from the olives by putting immense pressure on them. When immense pressure is put upon the beloved Son, His purity and love are squeezed out of Him. Gushing out with the great drops of sweat is His desire to obey His beloved Father and to offer His life for us.

There was never any question of Jesus disobeying His Father. He delighted to do His Father's will; it was more important to Him than food. **"Take this cup away from me. Yet not what I will, but what you will."** (Mark 14:36) With those words, Jesus took the cup from the Father's hand because there was no other way. Jesus said, **"Shall I not drink the cup the Father has given me?"** (John 18:11)

He was ready now to drink down God's wrath to its very dregs. Jesus made certain of His resolve by praying three times. Luke records that His sweat was like great drops of blood, and so the wrath began to trickle upon Him and would soon become a flood. **Then everyone deserted Him and fled.** (Mark 14:50) You cannot miss the rejection of the Son of God when He is deserted by friends, spat upon, handed over to the Romans and beaten within inches of His life, and then shamefully hung upon a cross to be jeered at by His enemies.

He was despised and rejected by men;

a man of sorrows, and acquainted with grief;

96

and as one from whom men hide their faces

he was despised, and we esteemed him not.

(Isaiah 53:3 ESVUK)

Immense as the physical sufferings were, the worst torment of all was bearing the full fury of His Father's wrath upon sin and evil. It was no mistake that led the religious leaders to hand Jesus over to the Romans for crucifixion. They accused Him of blasphemy, and the punishment for blasphemy was death by stoning. They were forbidden, by Roman law, to stone anyone to death, but that didn't stop them, as the stoning of Stephen in the book of Acts shows. They chose crucifixion for Jesus because the Law of Moses stated that: **... anyone who is hung on a tree is under God's curse.** (Deuteronomy 21:23b)

<u>He paid the price</u>

The priests wanted Jesus to be cursed by God, and in so doing, they fulfilled God's purposes. Peter declared this truth after the resurrection of the Lord Jesus. **"This man was handed over to you by God's set purpose and foreknowledge; and you, with the help of wicked men, put him to death by nailing him to the cross."** (Acts 2:23) The determined purpose of God was to pour out His wrath and curse His Son: **Christ redeemed us from the curse of the law by becoming a curse for us, for it is written: "Cursed is everyone who is hung on a tree."** (Galatians 6:13)

That verse needs a little explanation. To redeem means to buy back. It is used in the Bible for paying a ransom to set a slave or prisoner free. God gave His Son as the price to set sinners free from the curse of the law. As we have seen, the law was given not to make us good but to show how righteous and good God is. You cannot make yourself right with God by obeying the law because then you would have to obey it in full. Not just the letter but the spirit of the law, which includes your thoughts and attitudes. If you slip in just one thing, you are a lawbreaker. **For whoever keeps the whole law and yet stumbles at just one point is guilty of breaking all of it.** (James 2:10) Failing to obey means that the wrath directed at sin remains upon us. **All who rely on observing the law are under a curse, for it is written: "Cursed is everyone who does not continue to do everything written in the Book of the Law."** (Galatians 3:10)

Only one person could keep the law. The Lord Jesus was obedient in every way, and He, the only righteous man, kept the law completely. But He was cursed, as one who had sinned even though He hadn't. **Christ redeemed us from the curse of the law by becoming a curse for us...** (Galatians 6:13) **God made him who had no sin to be sin for us, so that in him we might become the righteousness of God.** (2 Corinthians 5:21) And so justice and mercy were both satisfied.

Charles Wesley, the 18th century hymn writer, said, "Tis mystery all: the immortal dies!" He was right; the death of Christ on the cross is an amazing mystery. It is yet another example of a paradox. The immortal Lord Jesus, the Son of God, gave up His life and died. Being without sin, He would not have died if He did not lay down His life or give up His right to be immortal. That is an astounding thought, isn't it? Many a tale has been spun around man's desire to live forever, and yet here we have a man who was not only eternal from Heaven but could have lived forever as a human because He never sinned. **"No-one takes it** [His life] **from me, but I lay it down of my own accord."** (John 10:18) He chose to die – He was born to die – to rescue us from the power and penalty of sin. The following story may help in illustrating what God achieved by the death of His Son.

When I was in my thirties, I had a little Honda 125 motorbike. I took an epic journey from London to Redcar in Yorkshire. I got there all right, but on the return trip, I missed my junction and got lost. It's tough being a learner on a motorbike, as there is no one with you to put you right and tell you not to take the first exit on the roundabout because that would put you on the M11, which would be illegal for a learner.

Well, I was alone and miss-read the sign and went on the motorway. I thought, 'I'm on the M11! No, this is the A10 – no, I am on the M11!' This was confirmed when the siren of a police car sounded behind me. They had followed me and mistook my panicked attempts to stop the bike as resolve to carry on. I did explain that I had made a mistake and I was lost, but that made no difference. The law takes no notice of excuses, I had broken it and so the police had to administer justice and I was fined.

Sometime later, I received an anonymous letter saying, 'Heard about your little adventure on the motorway.' Inside the envelope was the full amount I needed to pay the fine. I was guilty of breaking the law, but *someone else paid the price*. The law was kept, justice was done, but mercy was shown to me. By dying in our place, the Lord Jesus enabled the Father to administer His justice, deal with sin, and at the same time, He could display His mercy to sinners like you and me. Jesus is the One who turned the wrath of God away from us. **This is love: not that we loved God, but that he loved us and sent his son as an atoning sacrifice for our sins.** (1 John 4:10) The footnote of the NIV (1984 edition) gives the literal meaning of "atoning sacrifice", so using that footnote, the verse is saying: **This is love: not that we loved God, but that he loved us and sent his Son *as the one who would turn aside his wrath, taking away* our sins.**

The resurrection is essential to Christianity

How do we know that this message is true? The early disciples of Jesus were devastated by His death. The Bible is very honest in telling us that they went into hiding from fear of the authorities. To them, the world had just ended, and all their hopes were dashed. Left to themselves, the disciples would have gone back to their previous livelihoods. Over time, the story of the man from Galilee would have been forgotten. The religious leaders would have been vindicated in believing that Jesus was a liar and His claims of Divinity, the product of a deluded mind. There would be no Christianity because the followers of Jesus would be convinced that He wasn't the long-awaited Christ, the King who would free them from slavery. The Bible would not have a New Testament, and we would not be in the 21st century.

But we are in the 21st century because it is two thousand years since Jesus rose from the dead. Three days after His death, the tomb was found to be empty, and the disciples had an encounter with the living Jesus. The Resurrection of Christ changed everything. The followers of Jesus gave their lives in proclaiming that He was alive. The Bible records how Jesus taught them the significance of His death from their own scriptures, what we call the Old Testament. For forty days, the disciples met with Jesus, not eleven men but a group of men and women of about one hundred and twenty, and at one point five hundred saw Him at the same time. Ten days after Jesus ascended to Heaven these, once frightened, followers were dancing in the street and boldly preaching Christ crucified and resurrected. They witnessed a change in their lives which they attributed to knowing the risen Jesus. This has been the story of Christians from that time on to the present day.

The resurrection was inevitable because death could not keep a hold of Jesus

Death had lost its power. **"But God raised him from the dead, freeing him from the agony of death, because it was impossible for death to keep its hold on him."** (Acts 2:24) When there is a miscarriage of justice, and a person is jailed for a crime they did not commit, and evidence comes to light to prove their innocence, then the law must set that prisoner free. The innocent person can no longer remain in prison because, if they did, the law would be unjust. The power that held them in jail has been broken.

Jesus did not die for His own sins, but for ours. He had no sin, and that is proved by the fact that death – the result

101

of sin and penalty for sin – could not keep a hold of Him. Death had to let Jesus go because it had no right over Him. Justice had to release Jesus because He was completely innocent. His Resurrection was the inevitable consequence of His death on our behalf.

The resurrection means that we can know Jesus today

Jesus is alive! 'So what?' someone might insolently say. Are you kidding! This is the most awesome event in history! It means that everything that Jesus said about Himself and God is true! The resurrection affects you and me today. It means that you and I can truly know Jesus and share a personal friendship with Him.

Earlier I told you how I became aware of my own sinfulness when I read the Bible for the first time. What followed was a two-year struggle. I was reluctant to take it any further. I didn't want to become 'religious' or treat this as anything other than something to believe in without affecting the way I lived. God had other ideas, and in various ways, I came upon the message again and again. I met different believers who pointed me in the right direction.

I reached the point where I started going to church to find out more and making a real commitment to follow Christ. I wanted to obey that greatest of all commandments and show love to God and to my fellow man. I felt that God wanted me to become a minister, yet I still struggled with this increasing weight of sin and guilt. I would ask the church minister how someone who died two thousand years ago could forgive my sin today. He told me to have faith, and that just annoyed me.

God draws us to Himself in different ways and treats every person as an individual. He used my interest in science fiction. I was on holiday, walking along the walls of York, and thinking that, in another dimension of time, a Roman soldier was walking along that wall. Then I suddenly thought, 'God is outside of time. Time does not matter to Him, so it doesn't matter *when* Jesus died, but that He died.' Then I thought of the Resurrection. 'If Jesus has risen from the dead, He is alive today and able to forgive me now.'

That was the intellectual problem solved for me, and yet that immense burden of guilt remained to pull me down. I wanted to obey God but kept doing things I knew to be wrong. What could I do? What should I do? I was like the man described by Paul: **For I know that nothing good lives in me, that is, in my flesh. For the desire to do what is good is with me, but there is no ability to do it.** (Romans 7: 18 HCSB) Faith, that's what the minister said, but what is that?

I came to a point when the sense of guilt was unbearable. I felt I was suffocating under the load upon me. Then I simply cried out to God, 'Lord, take me and use me to do Your will!' That's all I did, I prayed and cried out for help. I didn't know it then, but I had turned away from my sin, rejecting it utterly and asking God to save me from it. As soon as I prayed that prayer, I had a picture in my mind of Christ hanging on the cross. I was looking over the cross from behind, rather like the Salvador Dali painting, 'Saint John of the cross,' or the image of the crucifixion from the 1959 film, 'Ben-Hur.' I 'saw' the blood of Jesus flowing

103

down from the cross and straight into my heart. Instantly, I felt clean inside, as if a refreshing shower had been turned on, and I knew, I really *knew* with certainty, that I was forgiven. I was forgiven because He had died for me.

I was given faith to believe that day. Faith is a gift of God. By faith, we receive this great salvation. I could not have believed if God had not revealed Himself to me. Through the Scriptures, through His people, He showed me that Christ is alive and that His death sets me free – more than that I am made right with God – righteous in His sight because of Jesus. And it was all because His Spirit revealed it all to me. **The man without the Spirit does not accept the things that come from the Spirit of God, for they are foolishness to him, and he cannot understand them, because they are spiritually discerned.** (1 Corinthians 2:14)

My lifestyle changed, and people noticed the difference. Even though I have been a Christian for over forty years, there is so much more to learn, so much more to this relationship than merely believing the message, and I will never reach the end of this amazing journey in this world. Even though we are freed from the penalty of sin, while we are in this fallen world, we are not free from its influence. I have made many mistakes I have frequently failed to resist temptation, I have had to ask for forgiveness of sin so many times I've lost count.

I have known very dark times – a Christian is not immune from suffering, but I know this: Jesus Christ, the Son of God, is alive and holding on to me, and one day He will present me holy to His Father. That is the story of every true believer in Christ, like the writer of Psalm 73:

**Nevertheless, I am continually with you;
you hold my right hand. You guide me with your
counsel,
and afterwards you will receive me to glory.
Whom have I in heaven but you?
And there is nothing on earth that I desire besides
you. My flesh and my heart may fail,
but God is the strength of my heart and my portion for ever.** (Psalm 73:23-26 ESVUK)

Chapter Seven

How we reflect the

image of God

This chapter is a bridge between part one and part two of Living Mirrors. We have tried to answer the question, who is God? We have had a look, more of a peek, at the Holy of Holies – God Himself. Much more can be and has been written about this awesome subject. The object of our look at God's attributes is to get an overall picture of His character, and the aim of that is to define what we mean when we say 'God'. Different religions and cults mean different things when they say, 'God'.

Who God is

An understanding, even a limited one, of who God is, helps us primarily to know God. You could read the previous chapters out of interest and even from the viewpoint of an atheist, or sceptic, and say that was all remarkably interesting. However, the purpose of the Bible is to reveal God to us, so that we can enter a personal relationship with Him. And who is God? He is: Beyond our understanding, all-present; One and yet a unity of Three Persons in One. God is eternal, self-existent, independent, all-powerful, all-knowing, and transcendent. He is love, Holy, Just, and merciful.

This is the Person revealed in the pages of the Bible and history. In the introduction, we looked at how God created us in His image, but in what way do we reflect the above? It is obvious that, in many ways, we are not like God at all. Even though the behaviour of some people can be baffling, no one is really beyond our understanding. Neither are we all-knowing or all-powerful, though I have met some people who think they are! We are limited to one time and place. We depend upon this earth for life. Our lives are limited; we came from the dust of the earth and will return to it.

How we are like Him

But there is more to human beings than dust. We have an eternal soul, a mind that lifts us above the animals. We reflect the Trinity because we are spirit, soul, and body. As God is the Creator, so we can be highly creative. We can rule over the world, meaning that we are responsible for creation and are meant to look after it. We think, we feel, and we can show true love. We need to keep in mind that we are reflections of God and not God. When humans were first put on this earth, they were good, without sin, perfect, and designed to live forever, but as we have seen, humans rebelled against God and so the perfect image was spoilt.

Spoiled images

It is because of sin that the world is in a mess and people do not believe in God. The spirit within us died, and we are born without a spiritual connection to our Creator. The main thrust of the Bible's narrative is of God's plan of salvation – His rescue mission of fallen humanity. The people and many events in the Old Testament point to the Saviour revealed in the New Testament as the Lord Jesus.

I believe that the reason we tend to reject God is because we do not want to face up to the fact that we are ugly inside. I didn't want to admit I was a sinner, which is why I took so long to surrender to Jesus. I think unbelief is not due to having a superior intellect or the evidence of science (many scientists are Christians) but a deep sense of knowing that what the Bible reveals is true. The sinful natures of us all make us hide away from God like Adam and Eve did when they first rebelled. The tragedy is that God longs for us to know Him and for us to be free, yet we resist His love.

The response

In looking at God, we have also looked at what He has done to save us from sin and its consequences. We have seen how the death of Jesus turns God's Just anger away from us. By His death and resurrection, sin is dealt with. But that is not the end of the matter but only the beginning. The most stupendous event in history demands a response from us, if we are to benefit from it. We are presented with a choice when we encounter the Lord Jesus Christ.

There are two choices, you are either for Him or against Him. This is a constant theme in His teaching, no one can be a spectator with Jesus; they either accept Him or reject Him like the two men who were crucified with Him. **One of the criminals who hung there hurled insults at him: "Aren't you the Christ? Save yourself and us!" But the other criminal rebuked him. "Don't you fear God," he said, "since you are under the same sentence? We are punished justly, for we are getting what our deeds deserve. But this man has done nothing wrong." Then he said, "Jesus, remember me when you come into your kingdom." Jesus answered him, "I tell you the truth, today you will be with me in paradise."** (Luke 23:39-43)

There we have the two choices starkly illustrated. The first man rejected Christ, so he remained in sin and under condemnation; **"but whoever does not believe stands condemned already because he has not believed in the name of God's one and only Son."** (John 3:18) The second man, however, repented. To repent means he agreed that he was getting what he deserved – the Just punishment for his deeds – and he turned away from sin, believing in Jesus. He knew that Jesus was innocent and more than a man. What did that guilty sinner see in Jesus; what made him rebuke the other criminal and declare Jesus King? It couldn't have been anything physical. Jesus' beaten body was not a pretty sight. On the surface, this Jesus had been utterly defeated. Perhaps the criminal had been impressed by Jesus' prayer of forgiveness, but though that could be true, it is not enough to make anyone put their faith in Jesus.

The explanation is simple: The Holy Spirit opened his eyes and revealed who Jesus truly was. Earlier, I quoted 1 Corinthians 2:14: **"The man without the Spirit does not accept the things of God, for they are foolishness to him..."** This is the first man, the whole idea of Jesus being the long-awaited Messiah was a joke. 'A saviour being executed – you've got to be kidding!' **"... and he cannot understand them, because they are spiritually discerned."**

One man was hard-hearted and deaf to the Spirit's voice, but the other listened and received the promise: **Whoever believes in him is not condemned** (John 3:18). And this is significant because it highlights the fact that we can do nothing to save ourselves. That criminal had nothing to be commended for. He could do nothing to make himself right in God's eyes – he was dying helplessly – all he could give to Jesus was his sorrow and his faith. Salvation is from God from start to finish.

> Nothing in my hand I bring,
>
> Simply to Thy cross I cling,
>
> Naked, come to Thee for dress,
>
> Helpless, look to Thee for grace...
>
> (Augustus Montague Toplady 1740-78)

There can only be one proper response to love like this: **Therefore, I urge you, brothers, in view of God's mercy,**

to offer your bodies as living sacrifices, holy and pleasing to God – this is your spiritual act of worship. (Romans 12:1) The only proper response is to turn away from sin and surrender everything you and I have to the Lord Jesus. Stop living for ourselves and start living for Him. This is summed up beautifully in my favourite hymn:

> When I survey the wondrous cross
> On which the Prince of Glory died,
> My richest gain I count but loss,
> And pour contempt on all my pride.
>
> Forbid it Lord, that I should boast
> Save in the death of Christ my God;
> All the vain things that charm me most,
> I sacrifice them to His blood.
>
> See from His head, His hands, His feet,
> Sorrow and love flow mingled down;
> Did e'er such love and sorrow meet,
> Or thorns compose so rich a crown?
>
> His dying crimson, like a robe,
> Spreads o'er his body on the tree;
> Then am I dead to all the globe,
> And all the globe is dead to me.
>
> Were the whole realm of nature mine,
> That were an offering far too small,
> Love so amazing, so divine,
> Demands my soul, my life, my all.

How we reflect the image of God

(Isaac Watts 1674-1748)

Declared Right with God

We are not just forgiven by Jesus' death; there is much more. Sin is no longer a barrier between the true believer and God. **There is no difference, for all have sinned and fall short of the glory of God, and are justified freely by his grace through the redemption that came by Christ Jesus.** (Romans 3:23-24) Justification means to be vindicated, declared innocent. God the Father presented His Son as the sacrifice that would turn away His wrath towards sin. **He presented Him to demonstrate His righteousness at the present time, so that He would be righteous and declare righteous the one who has faith in Jesus.** (Romans 3:26 HSCB)

God's righteousness and justice was satisfied by Christ's death, and so He now declares righteous – morally pure and holy – the person who puts their faith in Christ Jesus. God sees His Son. He sees all His goodness. He does not see our sin because He has declared us not guilty, and He has credited us with the righteousness and the goodness of Christ.

Imagine that you are in debt, and the bank has issued criminal proceedings against you. You are out of your depth, there is no way you can repay the debt, all hope is lost, and then you get a phone call from the bank manager, who wants to see you. Expecting even more bad news, you enter his office. He smiles at you, asks you to sit, and makes an astounding announcement. He has legally - with his own money - credited your account with millions of pounds. Not only can you pay off all your debts, but you can also live free of debt for the rest of your life. The bank manager becomes your mentor and friend to make sure you use your new freedom correctly and to avoid getting into debt ever again. When we have faith in Christ, relying upon His sacrifice, we are credited with His priceless goodness. **Consider Abraham: "He believed God, and it was credited to him as righteousness."** (Galatians 3:6)

Children of God

A popular misconception is that God is the Father of everyone in the world, but the Bible makes it clear that, because of sin, it is only those whom God has made alive in Christ, and filled with the Holy Spirit, who can call Him Father. Those who believe, not just intellectually, but surrender their lives to Christ in total faith in Him, are given new spiritual lives. Jesus called this being 'born again' or 'born from above'. **"I tell you the truth, no-one can see the kingdom of God unless he is born again."** (John 3:3)

The idea is that God's Spirit makes our spirits alive, and the change within us is as dramatic as being born all over again. Another word for this change is regeneration, which is not physical change but spiritual; our inner lives can now communicate with God, who adopts us as His children. **Yet to all who received him** (Jesus)**, to those who believed in his name, he gave the right to become children of God – children born not of natural descent, nor of human decision or a husband's will, but born of God.** (John 1:12-13)

But when the time had fully come, God sent his Son, born of a woman, born under the law, Jesus was born a Jew and kept the Law of Moses, the only man to ever do so, but he kept the law as our representative, **to redeem** (buy back from slavery) **those under law, that we might receive the full rights of sons.** In Jewish culture, it was the son who inherited the father's wealth, so here is equality for everyone who is adopted by God, as both men and women are treated as sons. **Because you are sons, God sent the Spirit of his Son into our hearts, the spirit who calls out, "Abba, Father." So you are no longer a slave, but a son; and since you are a son, God has made you also an heir.** (Galatians 4:4-7) In Christ Jesus, our new relationship with God is as elder sons who inherit the kingdom of Heaven. But that's not all; we are loved with the same love the Father has for Jesus: **I made Your name known to them and will make it known, so the love You have loved Me with may be in them and I may be in them.** (John 17:26 HCSB) This thought that 'I'm loved with the eternal love the Father has for the Son', simply staggers me. He doesn't treat me as the wretched sinner that I am but as His dear blameless Son! And consequently I, a sinner, can call the Holy, Almighty God – 'Father!'

As God's children, we will want to enjoy our freedom from the debt of sin correctly. We will want to make sure we don't deliberately sin anymore. And because we are not under the penalty of the law, when we do sin, and turn to Christ for mercy, we can be certain that we receive it. **If we confess our sins, he is faithful and just and will forgive us our sins and purify us from all unrighteousness.** (1 John 1:9)

Children are like the parent

When I look in the mirror and see my aging features, I see my dad. But I am conscious that I am also like him in other ways. I like classical music, I love reading and writing, I am told I am a pretty good cook like my dad, who was a professional chef. I reflect my dad's image because I am his son. In Christ Jesus, the image of God is restored within the heart of the believer, who becomes His child and reflects His qualities. God treats us like His son and indeed begins to make us like His One and only Son. But this process of being made holy is not instant, it takes a lifetime of walking in the Holy Spirit.

Part two of this book will look in-depth at how we become living mirrors reflecting His image and exactly what we reflect. I have chosen to study a passage in Galatians chapter five, where Paul speaks of the fruit of the Spirit. The fruit is the result of the Holy Spirit's work within us; it is the likeness of God reproduced within the believer. In simple terms, the Spirit's job is to make us like the Lord Jesus.

Part Two:

Becoming Living Mirrors

How Do We Reflect God's Image?

Chapter Eight

The fruit of the new nature

Warnings against legalism

The letter of Galatians was written to a group of Christians, who were being confused by false teaching, and this led to factions within the Church. Some Jewish believers believed that everyone had to obey the Old Testament laws and regulations to become true Christians, and a person wasn't truly saved from sin and eternal death unless they observed all the laws of Moses. The specific issue Paul tackles is circumcision, the removal of the foreskin as a sign of belonging to God. Like in the letter to the Romans, Paul argues that a person is not set free from sin by keeping the law but by faith in Christ and what He achieved by His death and resurrection. As we have seen in part one of this book, nobody can set themselves free from the power or the punishment of sin or make themselves right with God.

Only Christ can do that. We receive His goodness by faith alone.

The law shows us that we are sinners but cannot rescue us from sin. All the law can do is condemn us. God gave the law to reveal His nature and our need of Him. He gave it to show how we cannot save ourselves. The Lord Jesus came and kept the law. He lived a sinless life, was obedient to His Father, and fulfilled all the law, including the moral and sacrificial laws. To keep these laws, in order to be set free from sin, is to deny the power of Christ to rescue us. So then, non-Jewish believers were not required to be circumcised, abstain from certain foods, or keep the Jewish ceremonies and rituals.

Paul, like Jesus before him, was attacking legalism – the tendency to insist that believers do things in certain ways, keeping rules that are not necessarily found in Scripture. The religious leaders, called the Pharisees, had added many regulations to the Sabbath day, making it a day of fear instead of a day of rest, because if you didn't keep their additions to the law, then you could be expelled from the synagogue. Jesus' harshest criticisms were fired at these legalists and their self-righteous spirit.

Legalism can show its ugly head in many ways, such as only those who read the King James Version of the Bible are true Christians, you must only sing old hymns or only sing new hymns, or not sing hymns at all! You must confess your sins to a priest, have your baby christened or else they will not go to Heaven, pray to the saints, pray for the dead and observe certain rituals. You must attend every meeting in church, do nothing at all on a Sunday except read your Bible, only those who speak in tongues or raise their hands when singing are filled with the Spirit, never watch TV or go to the cinema, don't dance, don't drink, and so the list can go on and on. It was this mindset that Paul was challenging in Galatians. His position was that believers in Christ are not only set free from sin, but also from the obligation of keeping the *entire* Law of Moses.

Freedom to resist sin

However, we must be careful and not say that the law is no longer applicable to Christians. The moral law is still valid, and you may remember that it was given to demonstrate our love for God. Paul puts it this way: **You, my brothers, were called to be free. But do not use your freedom to indulge the sinful nature; rather serve one another in love. The entire law is summed up in a single command: "Love your neighbour as yourself." If you keep on biting and devouring each other, watch out or you will be destroyed by each other.** (Galatians 5:13-15)

We may be free from sin but not free *to* sin. If we rebel against God and do things that He hates, then we simply prove that we do not belong to Him. Love for God makes us want to please Him by doing what is right. **This is love for God: to obey his commands. And his commands are not burdensome...** (1 John 5:3)

Nobody can change their own sinful natures, but God can and does by the Holy Spirit. The death of Jesus brought in the new covenant; a covenant is an agreement between God and us.

**"This is the covenant that I will make..."
declares the LORD.**

**"I will put my law in their minds
and write it on their hearts.**

I will be their God and they will be my people."
(Jeremiah 31:33)

When we live according to God's way, we will prove that His law of love is written on our hearts. The law of God becomes dear to us, and our inclination is to obey Him. The person who loves Jesus as Lord cannot do the things they once did, nor do they want to. A new life means a new lifestyle where we begin to reflect the likeness of Christ. The Galatians were in danger of falling back into sinful ways, and Paul tells them how to avoid this: **So I say, live by the Spirit, and you will not gratify the desires of the sinful nature. For the sinful nature desires what is contrary to the Spirit, and the Spirit what is contrary to the sinful nature. They are in conflict with each other, so that you do not do what you want.** (Galatians 5:16-17)

The old versus the new

The Holy Spirit creates in us a new nature, free from the penalty of sin and free from slavery to sin but, because we still live in a fallen, sinful world, we are not free from the *influence* of sin. We must allow the Holy Spirit to guide us and direct the way we live if we are to be free from the influence of the old, sinful, nature. You cannot compromise with sin and try to please God and please your sinful desires at the same time because they are contrary and totally opposed to each other. A true Christian will not deliberately want to sin because they know the true value of the cross. The old nature is to be resisted because it is in conflict with the new. **But if you are led by the Spirit, you are not under the law.** (Galatians 5:18) The law of Moses contains two types of law. There are many ceremonial instructions, including ritual cleaning, circumcision, food laws, and animal sacrifices, and there are moral laws, including the Ten Commandments. The moral law can be summed up as: Love God and love your neighbour. When we are led by the Holy Spirit, we are not under the obligation to obey every little detail of the ceremonial law to be rescued from the power of sin, or to be clean from sin.

Paul goes on to contrast the old nature with the new one. The acts of the first nature give us a clear description of sin: **Now the works of the flesh are obvious: sexual immorality, moral impurity, promiscuity, idolatry, sorcery, hatred, strife, jealousy, outbursts of anger, selfish ambitions, dissensions, factions, envy, drunkenness, carousing, and anything similar. I tell you about these things in advance — as I told you before — that those who practice such things will not inherit the kingdom of God.** (Galatians 5:19-21 HCSB) This is the behaviour of those who do not know Christ. The secular world is opposed to God and tends to turn things upside down. The world calls evil good and good evil. There is a certain moral code, but it's based not on God's moral laws but on human opinion, so the things listed above may be acceptable to some people.

The person who has a new life in the Lord Jesus will know, for example, that sexual intercourse is something special and meant to be expressed in marriage between a man and a woman. In fact, the things listed above and other sins recorded elsewhere in the Bible will become hateful to the true Christian. By that, I mean our conscience will be more sensitive, and we will hate to do the things that would offend God and cause a break in our friendship with Him. When we grow as believers and become more Christ-like, we find that we hate what God hates and love what God loves.

The Good News of Christ is the means by which God turns enemies into friends, and we should be displaying the likeness of Christ to the world for people to see Him. This is the main point of Paul's teaching, in Galatians 5, that when Jesus lives in our hearts by the Holy Spirit, He will be seen in us. **But the fruit of the Spirit is love, joy, peace, patience, kindness, goodness, faithfulness, gentleness and self-control. Against such things there is no law.** (Galatians 5:22-23) Those who live like this are free from the condemnation of the law because they have the moral law written on their hearts.

Those who belong to Christ Jesus have crucified the sinful nature with its passions and desires. Since we live by the Spirit, let us keep in step with the Spirit. Let us not become conceited, provoking and envying each other. (Galatians 5:24-26) The true Christian is given a remarkable power – the power to resist sin and make a clear choice to walk away from wrong. Those who are in Christ have crucified the flesh. In other words, we have died to

124

sin and must count ourselves dead to this world system, which rejects God. Paul uses two metaphors to illustrate the Christian life. One is to walk; the other is fruit.

Walking in step with the Spirit

The metaphor of walking has been lost in the NIV, but it is suggested in the phrase, **Keep in step with the Spirit.** Other translations render verse 16 as: **But I say, walk by the Spirit, and you will not gratify the desires of the flesh.** (Galatians 5:16 ESVUK) Walking implies progress. We take a journey from one place to another, so our Christian walk is a journey from this world to Heaven. Walking also suggests behaviour because we talk about walking a certain way, in this sense, the Christian walk is the same as the Christian life – we live a certain way – one that pleases God.

Walking also implies effort. To walk, you need to stand up and put one foot in front of another. If you don't do that, you will get nowhere. The Christian life is not a passive one. We don't just sit back and let God do everything for us. When a baby is born, they have the potential to walk, talk, feed and clothe themselves. Babies come complete with legs, arms, mouths, and tongues! The potential to live a full life is there, but a new-born has yet to realise it. A baby develops slowly, steadily and the process of growing up is one of discovering what your mind and body can do.

Life is given to us; we cannot conceive ourselves. This is true of the spiritual realm. You and I can do nothing to save ourselves from the power of sin and evil – you cannot make yourself a Christian – it is the gift of life from God

Himself. We are made alive spiritually to God through Jesus by the power of the Holy Spirit. Now, when we have been made alive to God, we have the potential to be like Jesus; to live a pure, sinless life in a deep relationship with God our Father. However, we need to grow and make choices to actively resist temptation and imitate our Lord Jesus. **Therefore be imitators of God, as beloved children. And walk in love, as Christ loved us and gave himself up for us, a fragrant offering and sacrifice to God.** (Ephesians 5:1-2 ESVUK)

Being fruit trees

The second metaphor, the one we will examine closely, is bearing fruit. How do you know if someone is a genuine Christian and not just saying they are? How do you know that you are a true Christian and not deceiving yourself? Jesus said: **Make a tree good and its fruit will be good or make a tree bad and its fruit will be bad, for a tree is recognised by its fruit.** (Matthew 12:34) I am not very good at identifying plants and trees, but I do know that if apples are growing on the tree, it's a safe bet the tree is an apple tree. I also know that if the fruit is rotten, the tree that produced it is rotten too. **The good man brings good things out of the good stored up in him, and the evil man brings evil things out of the evil stored up in him.** (Matthew 12:36) The true nature of a person, what is really in their heart, will eventually surface in their behaviour, words, deeds, and attitude.

In the Bible, fruit-bearing and good works describe the same thing. They do not make you a Christian, but they prove you are. They are evidence that God has transformed you and is transforming you into the likeness of His Son. In other words, the fruit of good deeds is what is produced by the Holy Spirit living within the believer. It is something that God does within us when we have true faith. The two metaphors of walking and fruit-bearing are close companions; you cannot have one without the other.

We can't sit back and let God do everything for us. You can't say at your conversion, 'I've arrived! I'm like Jesus, so I don't have to do anything!' We need to cooperate and actively demonstrate goodness and love by what we do. **Suppose a brother or sister is without clothes and daily food. If one of you says to him, "Go, I wish you well; keep warm and well fed," but does nothing about his physical needs, what good is it? In the same way, faith by itself, if it is not accompanied by action, is dead... I will show you my faith by what I do.** (James 2: 16-18)

The metaphor of fruit-bearing also suggests dependency because to grow and bear fruit, a plant must depend upon the soil and moisture within it; likewise, true believers need to depend upon the Lord Jesus, who puts it this way: **"I am the vine; you are the branches. If a man remains in me and I in him, he will bear much fruit; apart from me you can do nothing."** (John 15:5)

Fruit for all

Just before we look at the fruit of the Spirit in more detail, note that I have been referring to the "fruit" singular and not "fruits" plural. A lot of people make the mistake of calling the example in Galatians 5 the fruits of the Spirit. Even though there is a list of nine qualities, they are all produced by the true Christian. The fruit is not to be confused with the gifts of the Spirit, which are abilities given to believers to serve God and one another. There are many gifts, and no believer has all the gifts. In contrast, *every* true Christian will bear *all* the fruit, for it is no less than a description of what a Christian is. God is seen in His children when they produce the fruit of the Spirit, which is the reflection of Jesus within us, making us mirrors of God's image.

Chapter Nine

Aspects of love

But the fruit of the Spirit is Love... (Galatians 5:22) Love... what is it? Is it merely a strong emotion, a good feeling? Love creates emotions, but that's not all there is to it. To many people, the word love equals sex. This is usually what the media mean when they use the word. Love, in pop songs, films, books, and TV programmes is mostly romantic love. Romance and sex are the most common understanding of the word love; this was brought home to me when I began to teach children. I remember telling a story, in a school assembly, and saying that Jesus asked Peter, 'Do you love me?,' and the children went into fits of giggles, some screwed up their faces and said, 'yuk!' From that time on I was careful to explain what the original word for love meant.

Empty promises

On the night Jesus was arrested, Peter had boasted that even if the other Apostles deserted Jesus, he never would – he would lay down his life for Him – he would never run away. It was a proud and foolish boast. Jesus then predicted that Peter would deny knowing Him three times before morning. And that is exactly what happened. When the pressure was on, Peter wasn't prepared to sacrifice his life for Jesus, not then anyway.

I would have hated to have been Peter, to watch my Master die a terrible death knowing that I had let Him down. I would have greeted the resurrection with mixed feelings of joy and regret. I would wonder if Jesus would forgive me. The guilt lingered on in Peter; he was unsure what the future now held. He returned to his fishing trade only to be frustrated with nothing to show for his night's labour. Then Jesus appeared on the beach and enabled Peter to catch an enormous number of fish. Once ashore, Peter and his fellow Apostles join Jesus for the breakfast He has prepared for them.

How deep is your love?

I imagine Peter kept avoiding Jesus' gaze and almost choked when Jesus called him by his old name, the one he was known by before Jesus named him the "steady one". (Peter means "stone") **"Simon son of John, do you truly love me more than these?"** (John 21:15) Peter's mind raced back to that fateful night when he declared a love greater than the other disciples and how he failed miserably. The Greek word for love that Jesus uses has the sense of choosing to disregard your own life to the point of giving it up to rescue another person. It is a totally unselfish love, prepared to put personal interests aside in favour of other people.

Peter knows that he doesn't love Jesus like this, he can't boast anymore, so when he replies, **"Yes, Lord... you know that I love you"** (John 21:15), he uses a different Greek word meaning friendship, affection, and fondness. 'Yes, Lord, You know that I care for You, I like You, I am Your friend.' Peter is honest enough to admit that his love for Jesus isn't as strong as death, but he declares his real friendship. Jesus then gives Peter the task of feeding His "sheep" those who will soon follow Him. Jesus asks Peter the same question, and Peter replies with the same answer, and so for a second time, Jesus tells Peter to care for His followers.

Peter's face must have burnt with shame when Jesus asked the question a third time, especially as He uses Peter's own words. 'Are you My friend?' This question is like an arrow in the heart, but it is an arrow designed to give life rather than take it away. Peter has no pretence now; his true nature is revealed, possibly with tears streaming down his cheeks, he declares, 'Yes, Lord, You know everything – You know that I am Your friend, and I care for You.' The command to care for His new disciples is repeated, so Peter is reinstated as leader of the Apostles. The three questions and answers cancel out the three denials, there is no lingering doubt that Peter is forgiven. Just in case we think that Jesus accepted a lower form of love from Peter, He indicates that Peter's love will become a deep, unselfish, sacrificial love, and he will indeed give up his life for Jesus and so fulfil a promise he couldn't keep before the Holy Spirit entered him. Read the full story in John 21. (I am using an outline found in an article on love from The New Open Bible Study Edition, New King James Version, published by Thomas Nelson. © 1990, 1985, 1983)

The Four Loves

English only has one word for love, which has several meanings, but the Greek used in the New Testament had four words for love. We will look at these words from the lowest to the highest concept of love.

4th Love: Erós

This is the origin of the word, 'erotic' and means physical, sexual love, the kind of love involved in romance. This word is avoided in the New Testament because of its negative associations with immorality. In the movies, James Bond is a symbol of the wrong use of erós. His 'love' is selfish, using women for his own ends. However, there is nothing wrong with erós when used in its proper place: marriage between a man and a woman.

The Song of Songs in the Old Testament celebrates this kind of love. That may surprise you that a whole book in the Bible celebrates sexual love because there is this misconception that Christians are against sex, but that is not so. God created sex when He made humans male and female. You read that in Genesis: **For this reason, a man will leave his father and mother and be united to his wife, and they will become one flesh. The man and his**

wife were both naked, and they felt no shame. (Genesis 2:24-25) This is how Adam and Eve were before they sinned against God, not after. They were 'one flesh' joined together in this physical expression of love, and there was not a hint of shame or dishonour about the naked body – that came after they had sinned. **Then the eyes of both of them were opened, and they realised they were naked; so they sewed fig leaves together and made coverings for themselves.** (Genesis 3:7) It was after the fall from grace that sex became corrupted. From the beginning, God's intention was that sexual union would be a beautiful expression of love between husband and wife and the means of reproducing children.

Because sexual love makes a man and woman 'one flesh', there can be no such thing as 'casual sex'. There is a bond between husband and wife that is more than physical, it's emotional, psychological, even spiritual, which is why divorce is so painful because those who were one are ripped apart. Emotional and physical damage can be caused by having many sexual partners. Those who live promiscuously are never genuinely happy or satisfied and that's because erós is a love intended by God to be enjoyed within a lasting marriage between a man and a woman.

3rd Love: Storgē (pronounced stor-gay)

This is family love, the love between parents and children, brothers and sisters. It implies a strong bond of affection and fondness. This word is often used in the New Testament to describe the love members of the Church should show each other. The Church is a family where strong bonds exist between true Christians. **Show family affection to one another with brotherly love. Outdo one another in showing honour.** (Romans 12:10 HCSB) This kind of love spills over into friendships and into the next word for love.

2nd Love: Philia

This love is brotherly love, affectionate love. In Revelation 3:7, there is a city called Philadelphia, which is the 'city of brotherly love'. Philadelphia in the USA is named after this city. As we saw above, philia is associated with storgē, but it goes beyond the family and speaks of the bond between friends. If you like someone and are attracted to their company, you are displaying affection and brotherly love. We tend to be drawn to people like ourselves, with similar interests and ideas, so it's good to know that God does not command us to *like* everyone. Being imperfect as we are, we would find that impossible. There is a selfish aspect to these three loves we've just described. They are loves that reward us; we personally gain from them, and they are strongly linked to our feelings. However, the highest word for love is totally *selfless*.

1st Love: Agapē (pronounced ag-a-pay)

Agapē was taken over by Christians and used exclusively for Christian love, and it describes a self-sacrificial love, where the will overrides emotions. Our emotions often control our love for family and friends, but this agapē goes beyond emotions and engages the will. In other words, we choose to love someone we would not normally like. You might not like that person, they may even have hurt you, but you choose not to harm them. You go further and choose to do good for them. This agapē love seeks to build up fellow Christians and reaches out to those who have no faith in Christ. This love is completely selfless, showing kindness without any thought of reward.

Jesus uses agapē when He commands us to **"Love one another. As I have loved you, so you must love one another"**. (John 13:34) It is agapē love He uses when He commands, **"Love your enemies and pray for those who persecute you, that you may be sons of your Father in heaven"**. (Matthew 5:44) It is the person who is being transformed by the Holy Spirit who can choose to love their enemies – even those who persecute them.

Choosing to love often means overriding emotions, especially when we are irritated. Someone has just done or said something to annoy you, you feel hurt, angry, "put on", "got at" and your instinct is to hit back. Instead, you choose not to. You feel misunderstood, but instead of risking an argument, you remain quiet – you let it go, and then you decide to show kindness to that person. So, your husband or wife has upset you. They probably don't know they have. The scene is set for a big bust-up. The next hour could be filled with shouting or a deadly cold silence. You have the next move. You can choose either to take up the matter, make yourself understood, or to forget it. You choose the latter and make a cup of tea served with cake and a smile. This kind of love **keeps no record of wrongs** (1 Corinthians 13:6).

This love was shown by Jesus when He washed the feet of Judas, the man who betrayed Him. He expressed it for the soldiers nailing Him to the cross by asking His Father to forgive them. It took Jesus all the way to a shameful death for sinners like you and me. Jesus expressed how powerful this love is by saying, **Greater love has no one than this, that someone lay down his life for his friends.** (John 15:13 ESVUK) And Jesus didn't only die for His friends, as we have already noted, He died for His enemies: **For while we were still weak, at the right time Christ died for the ungodly. For one will scarcely die for a righteous person—though perhaps for a good person one would dare even to die— but God shows his love for us in that while we were still sinners, Christ died for us... while we were enemies we were reconciled to God by the death of his Son...** (Romans 5:6,7,8,10 ESVUK)

It is this love that chooses others over ourselves – even over our own lives if need be, that the Holy Spirit makes alive in us. This is the Divine fruit we bear, and we willingly decide to demonstrate it. It is not easy to love this way as we will see, but this love is the beacon shining through our living mirror, and it radiates through the other three aspects of love.

Chapter Ten

Loving God

But the fruit of the Spirit is Love... (Galatians 5:22) A true believer in Christ Jesus will be marked by a powerful love for God. This love will fill us like a fountain of refreshing water that gushes out of us to quench the thirst of our fellow human beings. Jesus was asked which commandment of God was the greatest and most important of all. He answered by quoting from Deuteronomy 6:4-5 and Leviticus 19:18.

"The most important one," answered Jesus, "is this: 'Hear, O Israel, the Lord our God, the Lord is one. Love the Lord your God with all your heart and with all your soul and with all your mind and with all your strength.' The second is this: 'Love your neighbour as

yourself.' There is no commandment greater than these." (Mark 12:29-31)

<u>All of me</u>

I knew that I didn't love God like this, but I wanted to, and so I prayed fervently that I would love Him with my entire being. That prayer led me to Christ as my rescuer and leader. I still pray that this would be true of me. I desire to fulfil this command: it is the motivation for my life. It may take me my whole life, but it is what I strive for. I am not alone, for every true Christian, who has been made alive to God by the Holy Spirit, yearns to keep this command.

How do you know for certain that you are a real Christian and not just one by name? A true believer is in love with God. Is He everything to you? Do you want Him to be? Is your life driven with a passion to please your Heavenly Father? Do you assess choices by the way they will affect God? Is your relationship with God the most important thing in your life – more important than anything or anyone else? Is your belief in God something that has changed and affected your lifestyle – all your life and not just a tiny part of it? Are you prepared to live for Jesus? Are you prepared to die for Jesus? When things go wrong and you face very hard times, do you still love Him? Do you praise God even when you don't feel like it? Do you trust God no matter what the circumstances?

If the answer to those questions is a resounding 'Yes!' or 'Yes, I really want that to be true of me', then you are a genuine follower of Christ, which is what the word, "Christian" means. Those who long to love God with their entire self are producing the fruit of the Spirit. Make it your daily prayer to love God with all your heart, soul, mind, and strength. Love for God will make a huge difference to the way you live your life, and it will become a life-long passion, affecting every decision you make.

Fan the flame of first love

In the book of Revelation, the Risen Lord Jesus rebukes a fellowship of Christians in Ephesus for losing their first love for God. Their enthusiasm, their loyalty, and their delight in God had faded. It is all too easy to push God aside, especially in this crazy busy modern world we live in. So many things demand our time and attention that we skip reading our Bibles, neglect praying meaningfully, fail to meet with other believers, and miss regular church attendance. When we "Go with the flow" of this busy crazy Godless society, our love begins to die, and we become the same as those who don't believe. I saw a caption once in an ornate garden, it said, 'Only dead fish go with the flow.' Don't let your first love die, fan it into flame if it is waning, pray with passion that you will love God with your entire being, and live the life of a disciple of Christ and a child of God to keep that love alive.

W.W.J.D?

When my children were teenagers, they joined the craze of the Christian youth of the 1990s and wore little wrist bands which had printed on them the letters, W.W.J.D? You could buy keyrings, badges, books, cards, and stickers too. The letters stood for, 'What Would Jesus Do?' The idea behind these letters was to have a visual prompt in times of decision, especially when facing temptation. Looking at the letters was meant to encourage you to stop and think about what Jesus would do in certain situations, by remembering what He actually did.

For example, what would Jesus do when confronted with hostility? **"He committed no sin, and no deceit was found in his mouth." When they hurled their insults at him, he did not retaliate; when he suffered, he made no threats. Instead, he entrusted himself to him who judges justly.** (1 Peter 2:22-23) So when we face hatred, opposition, and hurt, we follow Jesus' example. We make sure we not only tell the truth, but we also keep clear of spreading malicious gossip. We do not retaliate in any way at all. Revenge will not be part of our vocabulary. Instead of uttering threats and curses, we follow our Leader's example and commit the matter to our Father in Heaven.

What should we do when seeing someone in need? How do we respond to the suffering of others? We do what Jesus did: **Filled with compassion, Jesus reached out his hand and touched the man** [with leprosy]. (Mark 1:41) We need to pray for compassion, ask God for wisdom to know how to respond to the needs of others. I do not just mean responding to a crisis aid appeal – though that is a good thing – I am referring to genuinely caring for those in front of us. Remember how James spoke of faith being demonstrated by action? His definition of religion isn't church ritual but practical care for those in need. **Religion that God our Father accepts as pure and faultless is this: to look after orphans and widows in their distress and to keep oneself from being polluted by the world.** (James 1:27)

What would Jesus do if there was an unpleasant house-hold task, like cleaning the toilet, to be done? There was a job that needed doing when the disciples were gathered to-gether for their last meal with Jesus. It was the equivalent of cleaning the toilet, changing a nappy, or some task that causes revulsion. The disciples didn't want to do this job; after all, it was the task of the lowest slave; a person con-sidered unworthy of joining them at the meal. Luke records how the Apostles were arguing which disciple was the greatest among them. Perhaps they were arguing who should wash their feet. There were no slaves present, only the twelve and their Master, so what did Jesus do? ... **He got up from the meal, took off his outer clothing, and wrapped a towel around his waist. After that he poured water into a basin and began to wash his disciples' feet, drying them with the towel that was wrapped around him.** (John 13:4-5)

Washing feet was a necessity in a time when people wore open sandals and streets were filthy with the waste from donkeys, dogs, and other animals. Because they re-clined at the table; no-one wanted filthy feet next to them as they ate. Only the Lord Jesus, the Messiah, was willing to lower Himself and do the job of a slave. Just think of the scandal created in the disciples' minds. Here was their host being their slave. Here was the King of Kings washing dirty feet! This was an amazing demonstration of love as it mirrored the great sacrifice Jesus was about to give, mak-ing Himself nothing to the point of dying on a cross. He is giving Himself to His disciples, even the one who betrayed Him, so our attitude must be the same. No task at home or church should be beneath us.

As far as I can remember, I don't think my children rushed to clean the toilet or the cat's litter tray, but they did volunteer to wash the dishes now and again. At least for a while, the little bands around their wrists helped them think how they could love God as Jesus did. Alas, W.W.J.D? was a passing fad, though the principal is still good. Look at how our Leader loved His Father and copy Him.

You may think, 'Well of course Jesus devoted His life to God – He was His Son!' We think it was easy for Jesus to do what He did, but I don't call His horrific execution easy. Let us not forget that our Lord is human too, and if you look carefully at His life, you will see a man totally in love with God. It was His delight to do the Father's will; He described it as His food, the thing that nourished Him and motivated Him. **Jesus said to them, "My food is to do the will of him who sent me and to accomplish his work.** (John 4:34 ESVUK)

The mark or the fruit of a true Christian is a powerful love for God. It is not sentimental or purely emotional but a choice to devote oneself to the Creator. This devotion is total and costly. The Bible gives us many examples, but I want us to look at just three that sum up the kind of love Jesus and His followers display.

First: Love for God is costly

The first passage is Matthew 10:37-39 where the Lord Jesus says: **Anyone who loves his father or mother more than me is not worthy of me; anyone who loves his son or daughter more than me is not worthy of me, and anyone who does not take his cross and follow me is not**

worthy of me. Whoever finds his life will lose it, and whoever loses his life for my sake will find it.

Many find this passage difficult to accept or understand. Jesus is not contradicting the fifth commandment to honour our parents. He assumes that we love them, but love for God comes first and must be greater than anything else, even to the point of denying ourselves the comfort of family companionship. The Lord Jesus demands absolute loyalty and if given the choice between God and those we love, we are to choose God. The image of someone carrying a cross must have shocked those who heard it first, for to carry a cross meant only one thing – you were being led off to die. Jesus demands that we die to selfishness and put the needs of others above our own, but there is also a challenge here to literally die, out of loyalty to Christ.

As you read this, Christians in other parts of the world are imprisoned, tortured, and murdered for their faith. Children watch as their fathers are gunned down in front of their churches. To become a Christian in many countries today means a death sentence. This is especially true of those who have converted from Islam, but it's not confined to Islam; communist countries and other fanatical religions also persecute true believers. Many believers have chosen to die rather than deny Jesus – that's how much they love their God.

Persecution of Christians is not confined to the history books, it is happening now. If you think I am exaggerating, look up Open Doors or Christian Solidarity Worldwide. In the west, persecution is more subtle, and the law is increasingly used to marginalise true believers. The book of Revelation warns us of trials to come, in which to be a Christian will cost us our lives, and the question is, do we love that much? Is He worth dying for? That's what the Lord Jesus is challenging us to display, a love that is willing to give up everything for the beloved. I do not know how I would react if someone gave me the same choice that my brothers and sisters in Christ are facing right now, but I pray that I would make the right choice. Loving God is costly, how committed are you?

<u>Second: Love for God is focused</u>

The second passage demonstrating the quality of love we display when walking in the Spirit is in Matthew 6:33: **But seek first his kingdom and his righteousness, and all these things will be given to you as well.** In its context, this verse is speaking of a complete trust in God to provide for all our needs. Instead of focusing on material things and wasting our lives in worry or the pursuit of pleasure, we seek God's kingdom, knowing that He will provide what we need. Our focus changes from self to loving God above everything else. Seeking His kingdom – His rule in our lives and ultimately over the world – becomes our main desire. We want God to be properly worshipped, and to see His goodness reign over us.

God becomes the focus of our lives, He is the first thought in the morning, during the day we seek to please Him, and He is the last thought before we sleep; in other words, this is a deeply personal relationship with our Father in Heaven. How much do you long for Christ's return? Are you living for Him or for yourself? It is deeply sad when a person has spent all their lives accumulating things and money only to leave it all behind when they die. The richest people in the world are those who know that real treasure is in Heaven, and the best thing about Heaven will be meeting God face to face. Love for God is an intense desire for Him and yearns to be in His presence.

Third: love for God is a delight

The third passage shows us a quality of love similar to the one above. It is from Psalm 37:4: **Delight yourself in the LORD and he will give you the desires of your heart.** As with the verse from Matthew, this verse in Psalm 37 could be seen as a means to an end. We need to avoid the thinking of the young convert who said, 'Look, I've been seeking the kingdom of God for months now, and I still haven't got all these other things!' Delight in God is the goal of our life, not the means of getting what we want. Delight in God *is* the desire of our hearts. Because He loves us so much, He looks after the whole person and will not only give us what we need but will also fulfil those desires of our heart that are in tune with His perfect will.

To delight in God means to enjoy Him. When theologians were creating a statement of faith for the Church of England, they wrote: 'What is the chief end of man? The chief end of man is to glorify God and enjoy Him forever.' (Westminster shorter catechism) The purpose of the human being is to glorify God and enjoy Him for all eternity. This is what we were created for. We were made for Him. We were made by eternal love; to be loved and love in return. We are truly fulfilled when we enjoy His company. This doesn't mean we cannot enjoy other people or other things but that we are only complete when we fully love Him like this. The ultimate purpose of our existence is to enjoy God; knowing Him intimately is the goal of Heaven. This world will pass away, and you and I will stand before God to spend an eternity delighting in Him. If that prospect doesn't thrill our hearts, then we must question if we really do have saving faith.

<u>Our proper response</u>

This is real Christianity, and what a difference we Christians would make in this world if we enjoyed God. Living mirrors reflect this perfect love for God; it is the evidence of the Holy Spirit within us. Sadly, to a lot of religious people, including committed Christians, God is simply a part of their lives, a compartment to be opened on a Sunday or at a Bible study. Prayer is a chore rather than a delight, something we do when we need some help. But prayer is an expression of this love, it is engaging with God in conversation, and we need to develop our prayer life so that it becomes as natural as breathing. We need to realise that God is with us throughout our day, whether at work, school, or home and that all we do is to be an expression of our love.

Love for God is a response. **This is love: not that we loved God, but that he loved us and sent his Son as an atoning sacrifice for our sins.** (1 John 4:10) God is the one who loves us deeply, and so completely, that He gave everything to save us from the power of sin. Our love for Him is a response to this great love for us.

146

Chapter Eleven
Loving friends and enemies

But the fruit of the Spirit is Love... (Galatians 5:22) The greatest commandment is to love God and the second greatest is: **Love your neighbour as yourself.** (Leviticus 19:18) We are still looking at the love of choice, the Christ-like love displayed by the true believer when walking in the Spirit. The love that the Holy Spirit produces within us is tough love. It is tough for two reasons. First, it endures. This love doesn't give up but will continue to move the one who possesses it to demonstrate it. Second, it is the toughest thing God commands us to do. It requires that we put aside personal feelings and choose to demonstrate love in return for hate.

Who do you love?

Of all the aspects of Biblical Christianity, forgiveness is the hardest to practice because it goes against our natural instincts. However, this tough love is like a diamond, it endures, it is hard, and yet it brilliantly shines out God's image. Those who love like Jesus prove to be His true disciples. We will be looking at forgiveness in greater depth later in the next chapter but first, let us define what Jesus meant by loving our neighbour.

We can have a very narrow view of who our neighbours are. What immediately springs to mind is the person who live next door or in the same street as us. A religious leader asked Jesus, **"And who is my neighbour?"** (Luke 10:29) To this religious leader, his neighbour was his fellow Jew, and he considered anyone who wasn't a Jew as an enemy. In answer, Jesus tells the famous story known as the Good Samaritan. A man, on a journey, is mugged and left for dead. Two religious men pass by on the other side of the road, but only a Samaritan stops to help. Samaritans were related to Jews however, both parties hated each other. Their animosity was historical and had to do with the fact that the ancestors of the Samaritans had intermarried with non-Jews. There was a religious and political divide.

We could substitute the Samaritan in Jesus' story for any race of people or groups we have been in conflict with or simply dislike. To those who first heard this story, especially to the religious leader, Jesus' choice of hero was totally shocking. It is the enemy who shows compassion towards a dying man saving his life. The message of the Good Samaritan is that we are to be neighbours to everyone, regardless of religion, race, or status, including our enemies. That does not mean we have to agree with them or embrace their beliefs. As Biblical Christians, we must hold to the truth that the Lord Jesus is the only way to the Father.

But we are to offer that truth out of love and not bigotry. The best way of demonstrating that Jesus is the only way is to practice His perfect love and show it to every other human being we come across.

We need to be honest with ourselves and admit it can be very difficult to get on with other people. Think of those you work with, or in school, college, or university; could you really say that you like them all? Do you find it annoying when a member of staff interrupts you? Isn't it maddening when the phone rings when you've just started some project or you're cooking dinner, especially when it's a persistent salesperson?

It can be tough dealing with miserable people when we are shopping, the member of staff, bored with their job, who never smiles and only grunts; the person who jumps the queue or the one who takes ages to load up their trolley. Perhaps where the most animosity is felt is within your own family. Brothers, sisters, parents, children, relatives, and in-laws can, at times, really irritate us, and we do the same for them! Fellow Christians are not immune from the people groups that can test our love to its limits; a local church can be a seedbed of repressed anger. I think one of the worst things is to be greeted politely by someone who clearly doesn't like you. The lack of love in churches is the main barrier to church growth.

Let's face it; people are hard to get on with. I saw a science fiction programme once, where a man was granted three wishes. He wished for peace on earth and everyone in the world, except for him, vanished into thin air! The fact is sin has spoiled human relationships, and it needs a miracle to sort us out. The message of the Bible is that the miracle can take place when we surrender our lives to Jesus. His Spirit transforms us – that's what conversion is all about – and when the Holy Spirit lives within us, He produces a love so rich, so strong and enduring, it heals damaged relationships.

The people of God, reflecting His love to each other

We use the word church to mean a building where people go on a Sunday to worship God but that is not the use the Bible gives it. The original Greek word, translated Church, means a gathering of people, specifically believers in Christ. Paul uses the illustration of the Church being the body of Christ: as each believer belongs to Christ, so they also belong to each other, joined by a spiritual union. I use a capital "C" when referring to this spiritual body, which is spread across the world, and a small "c" when referring to a local community of believers; in both instances, I mean people, not a building. The Church is an organism; not an organisation, the head; the one in charge of the body is Christ Jesus. Just as a human body has many parts with different functions, so the Church is made up of many different people, from all over the world, with varying abilities.

Another illustration could be a symphony orchestra, where different instruments make their unique sound but work in harmony with each other to produce a beautiful piece of music. When the orchestra plays what the composer has written, and the conductor interprets the notes correctly, the result can be outstanding. Christ Jesus is both the composer and conductor of the Church's message; when believers love as He loves, the result is amazing.

The Bible also alludes to the Church as a family, with individual believers being children of God, born again or made alive to God, by the power of the Holy Spirit; God is our Father, and other Christians are brothers and sisters. It never ceases to amaze me how I can be talking with another Christian that I have just met for the first time and yet feel that I have known them for years; this is the witness of the Holy Spirit within us. **The Spirit himself testifies with our spirit that we are God's children.** (Romans 8:16) I have been privileged to belong to fellowships which are interdenominational and international. This was true of Cliff College, the Bible College I attended, and of serving in the London City Mission. What mattered to us wasn't what church background we came from but whether we believed the essential doctrines of Biblical Christianity (the ones we've been exploring in this book). There was no need to engineer unity; it already existed because we were one in Christ Jesus.

Jesus said: **"Love one another. As I have loved you, so you must love one another. By this all men will know that you are my disciples, if you love one another."** (John 13:34-35) Jesus chose His followers to demonstrate His love to the world. The quality of their love for one another would be evidence of the Holy Spirit in their lives. They were being transformed into living mirrors that reflected God's love. Many people have become Christians because they were attracted by the lives of true believers. They wanted to belong to this group of people who genuinely loved each other and expressed that love in practical ways.

Loving all sorts

When I started to meet with other believers, I was impressed by the fact that I was meeting with people that I would not normally have chosen to associate with. God brings people together and enables folk from different levels of society to get on with each other. This was true when Jesus first gathered the Church together, calling twelve men to be His ambassadors. The twelve Apostles would not have chosen each other's company. Matthew (also known as Levi) was a tax collector. We don't like the taxman but in first-century Israel, tax collectors were collaborators with the Roman enemy, and generally dishonest; collecting far more than they needed to.

Jesus called Matthew to follow Him – a scandalous thing for a Rabbi to do. Now, that would have been difficult enough for the likes of Peter and Andrew, whose hard-earned money was taken by the tax collector, but for Simon the Zealot, it must have been humanly impossible. A Zealot was a freedom fighter, a passionate hater of Rome and anything to do with it. Zealots regularly attacked Roman soldiers in their effort to free their country. Simon would have considered Matthew a loathsome traitor to his country and only fit for stabbing in the back. Simon and Matthew would never have chosen to be friends or associate with each other, yet Jesus chose them both. He enabled them to change and love each other as He loved them.

The first Christians were by no means perfect, you only need to read the New Testament to realise that, and while we are in this world, the Church remains imperfect. There is no such thing as a perfect local church, but God promises that we will become the Holy people He intends us to be. Love is evidence that a church really is part of Christ's spiritual body. We know that we are true believers when we love other Christians. **We know that we have passed from death to life, because we love our brothers. Anyone who does not love remains in death. Anyone who hates his brother is a murderer, and you know that no murderer has eternal life in him.** (1 John 3:14-15) **Dear friends, let us love one another, for love comes from God. Everyone who loves has been born of God and knows God. Whoever does not love does not know God, because God is love.** (1 John 4:7-8)

<u>Actions speak louder than words</u>

How do we know if our faith is real? We will love fellow believers. There will be no hatred in your heart for anyone, even those, who in normal circumstances, you would avoid. This is love of choice. It is not sentimental, nor is it theoretical but practical and active. **If anyone has material possessions and sees his brother in need but has no pity on him, how can the love of God be in him? Dear children, let us not love with words or tongue but with actions and in truth.** (1 John 3:17-18)

In Jesus' story of the Sheep and the Goats, He makes it clear that those who belong to Him reveal their faith by practically caring for others. **"For I was hungry and you gave me something to eat, I was thirsty and you gave me something to drink, I was a stranger and you invited me in, I needed clothes and you clothed me, I was sick and you looked after me, I was in prison and you came to visit me... I tell you the truth, whatever you did for**

one of the least of these brothers of mine, you did for me." (Matthew 25:35-36 & 40)

Of course, it would be foolish not to accept that people without a Christian belief do charitable deeds on behalf of others, but there is a limit to human love. I am reminded of a pop star who raised funds for a famine in Africa in the 1980s. He continued his charity work for a few years until he announced that he was giving up due to 'Compassion fatigue'. Without the Holy Spirit, our love can only go so far, it is exhausting giving oneself to another person in need. But I am not talking about giving to charity – that is part of it – however, I want to impress upon us that the mark of a true believer is an enduring love that chooses to do good in practical ways to other believers and to people without any belief at all.

It is interesting to note that the word charity means love. It was the word chosen by the translators of the King James Bible to translate agapē – the love of choice. This love of choice will demonstrate God's love to everyone, even our bitterest enemies.

Chapter Twelve

No record of wrongs

But the fruit of the Spirit is Love... (Galatians 5:22) Magdeline Makola was a nurse from South Africa, living in Scotland when she went missing in December 2008. After ten days, she was found in the boot of her own car on Boxing Day, suffering from hyperthermia. Her attacker had forced her to give him cash from a cash machine, tied her up, and locked her in the car with no means of escape. A Christian, Madeline told the press that she felt no anger and had forgiven her attacker. On a website, she has said that she still forgives and prays for her attacker that, whilst in prison, he would change.

Gordon Wilson, a Protestant Christian in Enniskillen, Northern Ireland, hit the headlines in 1987 because he publicly forgave the IRA bombers who injured him and killed his daughter. When he was interviewed at the time, he said, 'I have lost my daughter, and we shall miss her. But I bear no ill will; I bear no grudge... It's part of a greater plan, and God is good, and we shall meet again.' When asked what he felt towards those who committed the crime, he answered, 'I feel no anger, I prayed for the bombers last night that God would forgive them.'

In October 2019 there was an extraordinary video of a scene in an American court room. Brandt Jean forgave the former woman police officer who was found guilty of his brother's murder. This very emotional young man said to her, 'I hope you go to God with... all the guilt – if you are truly sorry, I forgive you and if you go to God and ask Him, He will forgive you... I want the best for you... the best thing is to give your life to Christ. I love you as a person and I don't wish anything bad for you.' He then asked if he could give the woman a hug and that was granted by the judge.

The mark of love

These Christians and others like them refused to perpetuate hatred by actively choosing to forgive those who had wronged them. Of all the aspects of love, forgiveness marks a person as someone who walks with Christ, for to forgive completely is to be Christ-like. Just imagine the scene: The Master becoming the slave, kneeling at the feet of Judas. He takes a foot, filthy from the streets, washes the dust out from between the toes, and gently dries it. Then He reaches for the other foot, washing and drying that. In this simple act, the Lord was saying, 'I am willing to sacrifice everything for you, to lay down my life for you.' Jesus demonstrated this pure love to His enemy despite that love being rejected.

When He is arrested, Jesus gives us a beautiful example of His love and forgiveness. **Then Simon Peter, having a sword, drew it and struck the high priest's servant and cut off his right ear.** (John 18:10 ESVUK) **But Jesus said, "No more of this!" And he touched his ear and healed him.** (Luke 22:51 ESVUK) I love that detail in Luke's account that shows the deep compassion of Jesus even towards His enemies who had come with the crowd to take Him by force.

When flogged to inches of His life, Jesus does not curse His attackers; He remains silent. The Roman soldier at the foot of the cross declared: "**Surely this man was the Son of God!**" (Mark 15:39b) What made that soldier say those amazing words? He had watched Jesus die; he had heard no curses from His lips, only prayers and promises. Perhaps he was struck by the fact that when the nails were being driven into His flesh, Jesus prayed, "**Father, forgive them...**" (Luke 23:34a)

The central message of Biblical Christianity is that the death of Jesus Christ enables God to forgive the sinner. As we saw in an earlier chapter, God is both just and merciful. By dying in our place and taking the penalty for our sins, Jesus satisfied the Father's justice and mercy. The only condition for receiving God's forgiveness is to come to the cross because it was there that the price was paid. We don't deserve forgiveness, and we cannot earn it. It is a costly gift, freely offered to everyone. Offered to everyone but not received by everyone because, to receive forgiveness, we must admit that we are sinful and have offended a Holy God. We must accept the only way to be made right with God is through the death and resurrection of Jesus and believe in Him alone. **"Believe in the Lord Jesus, and you will be saved."** (Acts 16:31)

The act of repentance requires sorrow and commitment. To repent means to change one's mind and agree with God that we are sinners. It makes sense that the person who refuses to accept that they need forgiveness, and rejects Christ, cannot be forgiven. The story of the wasteful son in Luke 15 illustrates that God longs for us to return to Him and will accept us just as we are. **"I tell you, there is rejoicing in the presence of the angels of God over one sinner who repents."** (Luke 15:10) Jesus was a man who didn't merely practice what He preached; He preached what He practiced. **"He committed no sin, and no deceit was found in his mouth." When they hurled their insults at him, he did not retaliate; when he suffered, he made no threats. Instead, he entrusted himself to him who judges justly.** (1 Peter 2:22-23)

As we forgive

Because Jesus had a forgiving Spirit, He could teach us to pray: **"[Father] Forgive us our debts, as we also have forgiven our debtors... For if you forgive men when they sin against you, your heavenly Father will also forgive you. But if you do not forgive men their sins, your Father will not forgive your sins."** (Matthew 6:12, 14-16) At first glance, these words suggest that we earn the forgiveness of God by first forgiving others, but a closer look reveals that is not the case; we are not forgiven because we forgive – we forgive because we are forgiven!

Our forgiveness of others is part of giving up our self-ishness in repentance. Bearing a grudge is ultimately self-ish and leads to hate and evil deeds. 'I want them to pay for what they did to me!' If you don't give up that grudge along with all your other sins, then you can't receive God's for-giveness. Also, an unforgiving attitude betrays a lack of love. Forgiveness is the mark of the person who *knows* and *appreciates* that they have been forgiven at a great cost. The proof that God's Spirit lives within us is displayed by our love for others and forgiving those who have sinned against us. Even as those who follow Christ, we still sin and need forgiveness. How can we pray for that if we do not forgive?

Gordon Wilson, the man who forgave the terrorists who killed his daughter, died in 1995. Someone asked his widow, Joan, how he forgave them, and her answer shows that it flowed out of a life devoted to Christ. They had been married for thirty years, and every night for thirty years, they would kneel by their bed and pray the Lord's Prayer. When Gordon was in hospital the day of the bombing, he told his wife that they had to forgive; otherwise, they couldn't say the Lord's Prayer anymore. They both wanted to be able to pray, **"Forgive us our debts, as we also have forgiven our debtors."** (Matthew 6:12) In other words, they wanted to live out what they believed in and so for-gave the murderers.

Jesus told a story of a servant who owed a king a vast amount of money but could never repay it. The king cancels the debt, but the servant refuses to forgive someone else who owes him a small amount. The king asks the servant, **'Shouldn't you have had mercy on your fellow servant just as I had on you?'** (Matthew 18:33) If the servant had understood the generous love of the king, he would have forgiven his fellow servant. Because he didn't value the mercy shown to him as something to be treasured and shared, he was thrown into jail and tortured. Jesus ends His story with the warning, **"This is how my heavenly Father will treat each of you unless you forgive your brother from your heart."** (Matthew 18:35) God will leave us alone with our hardened hearts. Tortured bitterness is the result of an unforgiving spirit. When we do not forgive, we are imprisoned by animosity and rage, which destroys our peace, our health, our relationships, and is a barrier between us and our Heavenly Father.

No retaliation

Of all the things God commands Christians to do, forgiveness is the toughest because it goes against the culture of the day and our instinct to retaliate. It also goes against our sense of justice because we mistakenly think that to forgive means to let someone get away with wrongdoing.

This appears to be the meaning of 'turning the other cheek', but it isn't. **"You have heard that it was said, 'Eye for eye, and tooth for tooth.' But I tell you, do not resist an evil person. If someone strikes you on the right cheek, turn to him the other also."** (Matthew 5:38-39) Does Jesus mean that we are to literally let someone hit us again? Are we meant to let someone use us like a doormat? Are Christians prevented from going to the police and pressing charges when a crime is committed against us? No, of course not, that would conflict with a God of justice, so that cannot be what Jesus is saying.

What He is saying is: *do not retaliate.* The original teaching of an eye for an eye in the Old Testament wasn't a licence to harm but was intended to restrict revenge. Jesus makes it clear that the intention of that command is to make someone stop and think whether they should take revenge at all. If you turn the other cheek, you allow your assailant to stop and do what is right. By not retaliating, you offer a way to stop the incident from becoming worse. Schools tell children to walk away and let an adult deal with the one who hit them instead of engaging in a bloody fight. When you retaliate, you become consumed with anger and very often lose control, inflicting more harm than was inflicted upon you. A vengeful spirit is consuming, eating into a person's soul until they discover that their hatred makes them no different from those who wronged them.

Does forgiveness mean that we are to let people get away with a crime or an injustice? No, because by forgiving, you are handing the matter over to God, who acts justly. **Do not repay anyone evil for evil. Be careful to do what is right in the eyes of everybody. If it is possible, as far as it depends on you, live at peace with everyone. Do not take revenge, my friends, but leave room for God's wrath, for it is written: "It is mine to avenge; I will repay," says the Lord.** (Romans 12:17-19) The true believer is never to retaliate and seek revenge. We must flee evil in all its shapes and forms, and repaying evil for evil simply allows it to continue. Instead of retaliating, we must let go of hatred and let God deal with the matter. To avenge is to act on another's behalf to see that justice is done. In our look at the attributes of God, we saw that He is the Just judge who will *always* do what is right.

King Solomon summed up the role of God as a judge when he prayed, **"Judge between your servants, condemning the guilty and bringing down on his own head what he has done. Declare the innocent not guilty, and so establish his innocence."** (1 Kings 8:32) When an unbiased judge decides, in a dispute, he is not controlled or influenced by his emotions – a judge never takes sides – he makes his judgement on the evidence presented. In this way, the judge can be fair, reward the innocent and deal properly with the crime committed. Sometimes the law courts make mistakes, and a judge can be too lenient or too severe in their punishment, but God's judgement is perfect; He will always get it right.

There is a phrase that appears many times in the Old Testament, **"The battle is the LORD's."** (1 Samuel 17:47 b) He will fight on our behalf; He will right that wrong. He will clear your name if you have been slandered or falsely accused, you need to trust Him, and you need to forgive. Forgiveness is more than just letting go; it is the demonstration of God's love where we actively seek the welfare of the person who has wronged us. Instead of cursing, we bless, instead of inflicting harm, we do good. **"But I say to you, Love your enemies and pray for those who persecute you, so that you may be sons of your Father who is**

in heaven." (Matthew 5:44-45 ESVUK) **If your enemy is hungry, feed him; if he is thirsty, give him something to drink... Do not be overcome by evil, but overcome evil with good.** (Romans 12:20-21) This is tough love in action. Many people have given their lives to God because they were shown this depth of love by a true Christian.

Forgiveness transforms

Something happens to us when we pray for those who have wronged us; *we* change. When we ask God to bless, forgive, and pour His mercy upon them, then our hatred is turned to love and we see the other person as another sinner needing God's grace, just as we need it.

Whatever the situation we find ourselves in, whatever the hurt or injustice, we must let it go and forgive. I could give you examples of how I have had to forgive many times (and how I have needed forgiveness), but if I start telling you what someone did to me, then I am not really forgiving. We must not go over and over the matter in our minds or keep telling other people what was done to us or said about us. In unguarded moments, my mind can take a stroll down memory lane and turn that dark corner again. I remember what she said, what he said or what they did, and all the anger, hurt and bitterness resurface. In moments like that, I need to tell my mind not to go back. I need to ask God for forgiveness for holding on to the past. We can't change the past; we can't completely forget it either, but we can choose not to live in the past but to learn from it.

My wife has a saying: 'Draw a line under it.' She is a teacher and knows that when you draw a line under a subject you have done with it and you move on. Forget it, don't dwell on it, draw a line under it, move on, and don't return to the past. This is sound advice. When those unforgiving thoughts creep into your mind, shut the door on them and think of something else – think of Jesus hanging on the cross and dying to secure forgiveness for you and everyone else.

God has shown me a powerful aspect of His love that is beginning to transform the way I deal with hurts, misunderstandings, niggles, upsets, disagreements, and even wrongs committed against me. It is to put into practice something I want to highlight in Paul's description of love in 1 Corinthians 13. **Love is patient, love is kind. It does not envy, it does not boast, it is not proud. It is not rude, it is not self-seeking, it is not easily angered, it keeps no record of wrongs.** (1 Corinthians 13:4-5)

Deleting the file

Love... keeps no record of wrongs. This is the essence of forgiveness. The love of choice decides not to remember wrongs no matter how bad they are. Love will make you bite your tongue before you bring up an old hurt in a disagreement. Love has drawn a line under a past wrong and will not store it away. The human mind has an amazing capacity for storing memories, but the odd thing is we often remember the bad stuff more than the good. By not keeping a record of wrongs, we are not speaking of hiding the issue in the deep recesses of the mind and trying to pretend that it doesn't matter. Burying the hurts doesn't help us at all and can lead to all kinds of health issues, which is why psychiatrists and therapists will take a client over the past to make repressed memories resurface. But once the memory is out in the open, we need to apply God's grace to it and completely forgive. Like obsolete files on our computers, we need to delete the record of wrongs.

There is a story of a pensioner who read an article in a woman's magazine on how to improve her relationship with her husband. It advised not to bury resentments but to be honest and speak to her husband about them. It suggested that she and her husband should have times when they talk about the issues that upset them. The woman got two writing pads and pens. She told her husband that she was going to write down all the things that niggled her; things that he did that got on her nerves, like leaving the top off the toothpaste, not putting down the toilet seat, that sort of thing. He was to do the same, and they were to discuss the issues raised and promise to avoid upsetting the other in the future. The wife had a long list, read it out to her husband as he sat silently and nodded in agreement. 'Now it's your turn,' she said, 'what annoys you about me.' He handed his piece of paper to her. It had a short sentence on it. 'I can't remember because I love you.'

The husband made a deliberate choice not to be irritated by his wife's foibles. Love is patient, it is kind and it does not make a list of all the petty things that annoy us in life. It chooses not to misunderstand, not to be offended or upset. This applies to all relationships like husband and wife, colleagues at work, school friends, people we meet on a daily basis, and members of a church. Love will not rake

165

up the past. Love will not make a list of wrongs said and done. Love will be understanding and patient.

By not keeping a record of wrongs, we imitate our Father in Heaven for this is what He does with us. **"For I will forgive their wickedness and will remember their sins no more."** (Jeremiah 31:34) God chooses to put our sins and failures aside. He does not keep a record of your wrongs or mine – this is absolutely amazing! Do you have a hard time forgiving yourself? You can forgive others, but you dwell on your own sins, not just those in the past but the things you've done today. Have you confessed your sin and asked for forgiveness? Then you have it! Christ's death is completely sufficient to turn away God's wrath from all our sins past, present, and future. He does not remember your sin anymore, and neither should you. Do not keep a record of wrongs – not even your own.

The truth is we cannot completely forget the past, after all, our memories are part of us, and we can learn from past mistakes and triumphs. Forgiveness is not a denial of the past, but it is a choice not to live in it. It is a choice not to allow past bitterness to destroy today's peace and joy. Forgiveness not only allows us to move on, but it gives the person we have forgiven the opportunity to move on too, and to be valued as a person. Forgiveness demonstrates God's perfect love and benefits our mental, emotional, and physical well-being. Magdeline Makola, the nurse locked in the boot of her freezing car for ten days, attributes her good health, and the fact that she never suffered from depression or post-traumatic stress to forgiveness, leaving no room for bitterness of spirit.

Love: the most important choice you will ever make

Christian love is a choice. It isn't something you "fall in" and "out" of as if you have no control over it at all. That's a lame excuse for unfaithfulness. 'I don't love you anymore. I've fallen in love with someone else.' The simple truth of a statement like this is: you have *chosen* to reject your husband or wife. You have chosen to join yourself with another. You could have chosen to remain faithful, sort out any problems and seek reconciliation. You could have chosen to ask for God's strength to help you keep your marriage vows and chosen never to think of a romantic attachment to another person. When the tempter comes, and whispers in our ears, we can choose not to listen, tell him in Jesus' name to go away. **Submit yourselves then to God. Resist the devil, and he will flee from you. Come near to God and he will come near to you.** (James 4:7-8) The moment we give in to God, agree with Him that His ways are right; He gives us the power to resist the devil who will run away in defeat. The power of the cross of Christ is that He sets you and me free from the power of sin to be able to choose right over wrong. If the feelings towards someone close to you are fading, then why not choose to do something kind, practical, caring, and thoughtful for them?

Love is not an optional extra for the Christian; it is the essence of being children of God, for God is love. His Spirit produces love within the heart of the believer, and if love is missing then, so is God. A Christian is a person who loves God. A Christian is a person who loves others, including fellow Christians, non-Christians and even our enemies. Loving God and your neighbour is the most important choice you will ever make. In Revelation 2, the risen Lord Jesus rebukes the church at Ephesus for forsaking their first love. **Yet I hold this against you: You have forsaken your first love. Remember the height from which you have fallen! Repent and do the things you did at first. If you do not repent, I will come to you and remove your lampstand from its place.** (Revelation 2:4-5) The lampstand the Lord refers to is the church itself. If that church fellowship in Ephesus didn't return to their reason for being, then that church would cease to exist.

This wasn't a dull church at all. They had a great reputation. Jesus commends them for their hard work and perseverance in face of persecution; their purity because they did not tolerate wicked people and they taught the truth. And yet the most important part of being a church was missing. They had lost their whole-hearted, enthusiastic, devoted love for God and each other. Without love, they were nothing. **If I could speak all the languages of earth and of angels, but didn't love others, I would only be a noisy gong or a clanging cymbal. If I had the gift of prophecy, and if I understood all of God's secret plans and possessed all knowledge, and if I had such faith that I could move mountains, but didn't love others, I would be nothing. If I gave everything I have to the poor and even sacrificed my body, I could boast about it; but if I didn't love others, I would have gained nothing.** (1 Corinthians 13:1-3 NLT)

'[Love] is the most important thing about being a Christian – full stop... When you and I stand before the judgment seat of Christ to give an account of how we have lived our lives, Jesus will not be a bit interested in our competence. He will not be interested in how respected we are, whether we have reached a high position within the church or in the world... He will be interested in one thing – the first question He will ask is: how much have you *loved*?' Dr. Jeremy McQuoid.

Chapter Thirteen

Experiencing Joy and Peace in a World of Darkness

But the fruit of the Spirit is...joy, peace... (Galatians 5:22) I have never forgotten a story I heard many years ago in 1979. I don't remember the preacher who told the story or all the details; what I do remember was it was set some time at the turn of the last century before the age of benefits when a woman had to depend on her husband to provide everything. I have forgotten the names, so I'll make them up. Alice and her husband, Tom, lived in Yorkshire and Tom worked down the mine. He was a drunkard and had a terrible reputation for violence. His workmates kept their distance as they knew the least provocation could result in a fractured jaw.

Alice clung to the pittance her husband gave her to feed her starving children. Tom spent all the money on beer, so they went without basic things like beds and chairs. Alice had a miserable existence. An evangelist came to the little town where this couple lived. There was a revival of faith through the preaching of God's word, and many were touched by the Holy Spirit. By God's grace, Tom found himself at one of the meetings. He may have gone to jeer and heckle, but he felt the presence of God. The message of the cross touched his heart, and he responded to the message to repent and believe. His whole life changed; he stopped drinking, swearing and was gentle and kind. He soon became known as a faithful churchgoer and committed Christian.

Down in the mine one day, his workmates decided to test this newfound faith. They made jokes about religion, teased him, and said things that, in the past, would have landed them in hospital. One man shouted, 'I hear that your new gaffer can turn water into wine!' Tom put down his pickaxe and looked the man directly in the eyes and said, 'I don't know much about that, but I do know He can change beer into furniture!'

Tom's transformed life meant that he now provided for his family. The story does not record Alice's reaction, but it doesn't take a vast imagination to realise that joy and peace had replaced her fear and trembling. Joy and peace result from God's mercy being given to us. The miracle of being made alive to God and adopted as His child drives away fear and despair. The new convert knows this joy that is shared by the angels in Heaven. And this is the experience of all true believers in Christ even in tough times.

And though I told you a story from the last century, I could have told you many others; because God is still transforming the lives of drug addicts, alcoholics, sex addicts, the violent, the extrovert and the introvert, the criminal and the religious. These miracles of conversion are not generally reported by the media unless the person is a celebrity, but they are happening across the world every day. Many can tell how they had sadness turned to joy and unrest and fear replaced by peace.

The reality of suffering

However, we cannot deny the fact of suffering. Christians are not immune to pain. The teaching that when we come to Jesus all our problems are waved away as if by magic, is false. The so-called Prosperity Gospel is a lie. Beware of those who tell you that health and wealth are guaranteed to the Christian. Read Psalm 73, a prayer of a Godly man who wonders why the wicked have prosperous lives while God's people suffer. Physical and material well-being are not promised or given to all. Our Lord lived a simple life with no fixed abode, and He suffered *because* He was faithful to God.

Many of you reading these words may be going through a particularly tough time. At this moment, your prayers appear to be unheard. Your pain is great, and life is like stumbling about in a dark cave filled with venomous snakes.

Your feelings are overwhelming, and the idea that you can experience joy and peace seems utterly ridiculous.

I have lost count of how many times I have heard a statement like this: 'I can't believe in God because there's so much suffering in the world.' People stumble because they cannot understand how a God of love allows suffering to continue, so they give up on God. Some Christians believe that to experience joy and peace in this world is unrealistic. Some think that joy and peace are only to be found in Heaven. But the fruit of the Spirit is produced within the hearts of believers *now*. Paul is not speaking of some future state of perfection, he is telling his readers to live in the Spirit here and now, in this present evil age, as proof of a transformed life. The fruit of the Spirit is a description of every true believer in Christ in every age. Joy and peace are present possessions for all believers, not just a privileged few.

In 2 Corinthians, Paul tackles boastful Christians by boasting, not of his achievements, but of the afflictions he suffered as a servant of Christ. After his list of woes, and after describing an ecstatic vision, Paul goes on to speak of his 'thorn in the flesh'. He never tells us what it is. Whatever it is, this 'thorn' is personally and deeply distressing. He pleads three times for the Lord Jesus to remove this affliction, but his prayer is answered in another way, with a promise: **"My grace is sufficient for you, for my power is made perfect in weakness."** (2 Corinthians 12:9)

The answer was that He would not take Paul's pain away, but He would give him the strength to endure it. I want to thank the Holy Spirit for guiding Paul not to name

174

his pain. Because the source of his pain could be anything, what Jesus says to him applies in all situations of suffering. It doesn't matter if the suffering is seen as great or small, the fact is, suffering is suffering; pain is pain.

Invisible pain

We tend to compare our sufferings with those of others. This leads us to make unfair assumptions about another person's capacity to bear the pain. 'Well I don't understand why he/she is making such a fuss over it – he/she is not as bad as so and so.' One of the other unwise things people say is: 'Look on the bright side, there's always somebody worse off than you.' Strange comfort that! As if I should be happy at the thought of someone else suffering more than myself. We find it easier to have sympathy with obvious forms of suffering like the effects of a disaster or a physical condition. However, when it comes to invisible pain, either physical, mental, or emotional, we can fail to understand why a person is struggling with everyday life.

I think the cruellest example of assuming that a person is okay is in the area of bereavement. When someone suffers the loss of a loved one, there is an immediate sympathy for them, but that disappears a month after the funeral. Because we don't see the inner grief, we assume all is well. The cruellest thing to say is something like: 'You should be over it by now.' We move on when the bereaved person still has to live with their loss. Unless we are sensitive, we can easily forget that they are vulnerable.

It is a useless and often cruel exercise comparing pain and trying to quantify it. True compassion understands that

175

your pain, whatever it is caused by, is distressing to *you* even if I have never experienced that particular form of suffering. The good news is that there is someone who completely understands what you are going through. Whatever stage you are at in handling your pain, whatever you are going through, regardless of how dark it is, the grace of the Lord Jesus Christ is sufficient for you. You don't understand it, you may never understand why this is happening to you, but you can completely rely on the fact that He is right there in the darkness with you. He is giving you the strength and all you need to endure your personal 'thorn in the flesh'.

Not alone

During a very distressing and intensely painful time, I said to God, 'I'm in the dark Lord, I can't feel You. I can't hear You. I don't understand it at all, and I can't cope.' In answer, a line from Psalm 139 entered my mind:

If I say, "Surely the darkness will hide me

and the light become night around me,

even the darkness will not be dark to you;

the night will shine like the day,

for darkness is as light to you.

(Psalm 139:11-12)

My Father in Heaven was telling me, 'I see you. I am with you. I am holding you.' My mind wandered on to Jesus hanging on the cross. Darkness suffocated the land for

176

three hours and wrapped itself around the Son of Man. Jesus knows what it is like to be in the dark. He knew what it was to cry out in pain, knowing separation from the Father. We can never fully appreciate what God went through, the day the Trinity suffered a breach in fellowship and the 'immortal died'. I knew – without a doubt – that Jesus was with me in the darkness, keeping final despair far from me.

At that time, someone said to me, 'I don't understand how you still hold on to God with all you've been through.' I answered, 'Because He is holding on to me!' I didn't feel it, but I knew it was true. My doctor at the time told me, 'You will never be the same again, and your faith will never be the same again.' The implication was that I would lose my faith. I pondered on his statement and when I saw him a week later. I told him, 'You are right, my faith will never be the same again because it is stronger now than it ever was before. God is the only one I trust, the only one who makes any sense.' This doesn't make me a 'super-saint'. I could only say this because His grace was sufficient for me.

But is it possible to know and display joy and peace in a world torn apart by pain? The answer is yes; every true believer in Christ can experience the fruit of joy and peace from the source of joy and peace. Joy, as we know, is a deep-seated happiness. It is a very powerful, wonderful emotion that bubbles out of us with enthusiasm. The Hebrew word for peace is Shalom, which means wholeness or completeness. It refers to being in harmony and at peace with God, ourselves and others. These are not superficial

emotions but tangible strengths flowing out of our relationship with God. The question is *how* do we experience joy
and peace in a world of pain and suffering? This is such an
important subject that the next chapter will deal with suffering in depth, looking at the ways we are able to know
joy and peace in a world of suffering and darkness.

Chapter Fourteen

How to know Joy and Peace in a
World of Darkness

But the fruit of the Spirit is...joy, peace... (Galatians 5:22) Joy and peace are given to the believer by the Holy Spirit, and they are to be experienced now, not just in the future. But, how in a world of darkness and suffering, can we truly know joy and peace? These are subjective qualities. In other words, they are part of our feelings, they come from within, and they are something we experience. The reality is that when we are confronted with suffering and pain, our feelings are very different. Joy and peace fly away when tough times come. And yet it is possible to know deep joy and deep peace when we are walking in the Spirit – whatever the circumstances.

To experience joy and peace, we need to be objective. In other words, we need to look outside ourselves to God.

Paul was in prison for his faith in Jesus and knew that his death was approaching when he wrote: **Rejoice in the Lord always. I will say it again: Rejoice!** (Philippians 4:4) He had experienced intense suffering, and yet, he was able to rejoice, not in the pain and suffering, but in the *Lord*. He looked outside himself and looked upon the Lord Jesus and all that He is. Paul knew that he belonged to Christ, and he rejoiced in this wonderful person. To experience the kind of joy and peace Paul had, I suggest we practice four things to help us be objective in times of pain and suffering.

1: Cling to the promises of God

God is completely trustworthy. He always keeps His word. Faith is taking God at His word. On the night before the crucifixion, Jesus told the disciples about His impending death and resurrection, but at the time, they did not understand His words. He urged them to keep trusting the Father and Himself. He told them to abide in Him, and then they would bear much fruit. His relationship with the Father is the source of His joy. He taught them that they, and all who were later to believe in Him, would share that joy by entering into fellowship with the Father. **"I have told you this so that my joy may be in you and that your joy may be complete."** (John 15:11) This promise is that we will know the joy of Jesus. It is *His* joy, resulting from a love relationship with the Father, through the Son, and in the Holy Spirit.

Jesus' death and resurrection enable us to share in His joy. But the thought of their master leaving them brings the disciples great sadness. **"I tell you the truth, you will**

weep and mourn while the world rejoices. You will grieve, but your grief will turn to joy. A woman giving birth to a child has pain because her time has come; but when her baby is born, she forgets the anguish because of her joy that a child is born into the world. So, with you; now is your time of grief, but I will see you again and you will rejoice, and no-one will take away your joy. (John 16:20-21) What a great promise this is! No one can take away our joy! Jesus prayed for His disciples (including us). **"I am coming to you** [God the Father] **now, but I say these things while I am still in the world, so that they may have the full measure of my joy within them.** (John 17:13)

Another promise of Jesus is: **"Peace I leave with you; my peace I give you. I do not give to you as the world gives. Do not let your hearts be troubled and do not be afraid."** (John 14:27) By focusing on our Saviour, we experience the joy and peace He provides. Jesus was a man of peace. By that, I not only mean that He avoided violence but that He also demonstrated His completeness as a person. When He stood and faced the mob sent to arrest Him, Jesus didn't fall apart; He was calmly in control. His peace emanated from within when He was falsely accused and mistreated by the religious leaders. Pilate was a stubborn man so the history books tell us. He was decisive even when making a mistake, but when faced with Jesus, he procrastinated. He put off his final decision and was clearly unnerved by the presence of this man from Galilee. It must have been the fact that Jesus was in control. There was an unearthly peace about this man who never once pleaded for His life and didn't grovel at Pilate's feet. Even the beating and the cruel mockery at the hands of the soldiers could not dislodge His peace. No wonder Pilate declared: **"Behold the Man!"** (John 19:5 ESVUK)

In times of crisis, we are promised the very peace of the Lord Jesus, and this peace will keep us from utter destruction. All we need to do to have this peace is ask for it. **Do not be anxious about anything, but in everything, by prayer and petition, with thanksgiving, present your requests to God. And the peace of God, which transcends all understanding, will guard your hearts and your minds in Christ Jesus.** (Philippians 4:6-7) To receive the joy and peace of Christ, we must cling to the promises of God while trusting in His purpose.

2: Trust in the purpose of God

And we know that in all things God works for the good of those who love him, who have been called according to his purpose. (Romans 8: 28) And what is God's purpose? **For those God foreknew he also predestined to be conformed to the likeness of his Son...** (Romans 8:29) This is God's plan for true Christians: to be living mirrors, reflecting the likeness of Jesus – to become like Jesus and to be made fit for living with God in glory. He uses all things, the good, the bad, and the ugly, to serve His purpose for us.

We need to be clear that God does not cause evil. He is not the one who makes us suffer, but He does allow it. The process of making us perfect starts now but ends when we are in Heaven. We see in the Bible how God uses trials like a sculptor to chip off the rough edges from His chosen people to form a perfect image. We could go through the whole Bible and look at different men and women whom God made holy through suffering. However, we'll just look at two very different men.

Jacob's struggles with God

Jacob had been chosen to inherit the promises of Abraham. He was to be the father of a nation. But Jacob was devious; he deceived his father, Isaac, and cheated his elder brother out of his inheritance. We wouldn't have considered Jacob a man of God at all. But God met him and promised him, **"All peoples on earth will be blessed through you and your offspring. I am with you and will watch over you wherever you go, and I will bring you back to this land. I will not leave you until I have done what I have promised you."** (Genesis 28:14b – 15)

Jacob's prayer, when he received this promise, reveals a man used to bargaining, a person without full trust in God, a proud man impure and full of deceit. **"If God will be with me and will watch over me on this journey I am taking and will give me food to eat and clothes to wear so that I return safely to my father's house, then the LORD will be my God..."** (Genesis 28:20-21) He would only follow the God of his grandfather Abraham and father Isaac if God did certain things for him.

Jacob was used to getting his own way and what he needed was a dose of his own medicine. God started to chip off Jacob's rough edges when he met his uncle. Uncle Laban was a clever, subtle, and experienced cheat. In many ways, he was an older version of Jacob. Jacob falls in love with Laban's youngest daughter and promises to work for seven years without pay, if he could marry Rachel. The old man agrees, and Jacob slaves away for seven years. On the wedding night, Laban swaps Rachel for his eldest daughter, who is not as pretty and more to the point, whom Jacob does not love. We may ask how this is possible, but she would have been wearing a veil and been complicit in the deception because she had no choice but to obey her father. The next day Jacob complains and is told that he can marry Rachel too, on the condition that he works for another seven years without pay.

It's not looking good for Jacob. He has two wives, Rachel, whom he loves, and Leah, whom he doesn't, and it is the latter who bears him children, while the former is unable to conceive. The rivalry between the two sisters results in all kinds of schemes to gain Jacob's favour and bear children. Eventually, Rachel gives birth to Joseph; and Jacob, fed up with all the things his uncle does to make life difficult, decides to leave and go back to his father. It would mean facing his brother, but Jacob sets off.

When he hears that his brother is approaching with an army of four hundred men, Jacob prays. **"O God of my father Abraham, God of my father Isaac, O LORD ... I am unworthy of the kindness and faithfulness you have shown your servant... Save me, I pray from the hand of my brother Esau, for I am afraid he will come and attack me, and also the mothers with their children. But you have said, 'I will surely make you prosper and will**

make your descendants like the sand of the sea, which cannot be counted.'" (Genesis 32:9-13)

The tone of this prayer is very different from the one he prayed before he suffered at the hands of Laban. There's no pride now. It has been replaced by a humble trust. He reminds himself of the promise of God, but there is no bargaining, just a plea for help. That night, when on his own, Jacob wrestles in prayer with God, an angel appears to him and literally wrestles with him. Jacob will not let go until God blesses him. He realises after, that he has seen God face to face, especially as God changes his name to Israel, meaning one who struggles with God. Jacob's prayer is answered. He faces other trials and after each one, is more dependent upon the LORD. God used Jacob's many trials to remove his sinfulness and make him into a man of God.

The good man who suffered

Job was a good man who served God faithfully. That's not just my opinion; it is what God says about him. **"Have you considered my servant Job? There is no-one on earth like him; he is blameless and upright, a man who fears God and shuns evil."** (Job 1:8) Satan challenges this statement; he suggests that Job only loves God for the things he has been given, and if God took it all away, Job would curse him to His face. So God allows Satan to take everything away from Job. In one appalling day, all Job's children are killed in a storm, his property is destroyed or stolen, most of his servants are slaughtered, and all his wealth is wiped out.

But Job does not curse God; he falls to the ground in *worship* saying, **"Naked I came from my mother's womb and naked I shall depart. The LORD gave, and the LORD has taken away; may the name of the LORD be praised."** (Job 1:21) Satan is not satisfied. He says it would be different if Job suffered physical pain, so God allows Satan to inflict Job's body with painful boils from head to toe. He becomes an outcast, shunned by family and living in the rubbish dump. Satan continues to torment Job but in the subtle form of his friends who come initially to comfort him. However, these friends believe that Job has brought all this pain upon himself, through sinful deeds.

"May the day of my birth perish, and the night it was said, 'A boy is born!'" (Job 3:3) Though he cries out in anguish, wishing that he had never been born, Job's faith in God remains intact, and he never once curses God. He is the only one in the book to talk directly to God. The others talk *about* God, but Job talks *to* Him, and he is honest about his feelings, telling God exactly what he thinks. He does sin by becoming self-righteous and arrogant; however, he changes after God speaks to him.

During his torment, Job's faith becomes stronger, and he declares: **"Even if He kills me, I will hope in Him. I will still defend my ways before Him."** (Job 13:15 HCSB) **"But I know my living Redeemer, and He will stand on the dust at last. Even after my skin has been destroyed, yet I will see God in my flesh."** (Job 19:25-26 HCSB)

With these remarkable words, Job reveals a belief in a resurrection and a complete trust in God his rescuer. As a result of his suffering, Job's faith increases. He knows that death is not the end, and He will see God face to face. This next statement shows that Job can see God's purpose in all the pain: **"Yet He knows the way I have taken; when He has tested me, I will emerge as pure gold."** (Job 23:10 HCSB)

Gold is super-heated until it melts. All the impurities within the metal rise to the surface to be skimmed off. What is left is pure and precious. The purpose of God is to make us into pure and precious children, fit for living in His holy presence. God used pain to reveal what was in Job's heart; he didn't curse God, but he did need to repent of his pride, and so he was a better man after the intense torment than he was before.

The purpose of suffering

It is often in trials that our true nature comes out, and we discover if we are true Christians or not. Do we praise God or criticise Him? Does our faith in Him grow or die? Do we regard Him as cruel, or do we still love Him? Peter wrote to persecuted Christians who rejoiced because they could see beyond their pain. **In this, you greatly rejoice, though now for a little while you may have had to suffer grief in all kinds of trials. These have come so that your faith – of greater worth than gold, which perishes even though refined by fire – may be proved genuine and may result in praise, glory, and honour when Jesus Christ is revealed. Though you have not seen him, you love him; and even though you do not see him now, you believe in him and are filled with an inexpressible and glorious joy, for you are receiving the goal of your faith, the salvation of your souls.** (1 Peter 1:6-9)

Knowing that God's purpose is to save us from all evil and make us like His Son should fill our hearts with a joy we cannot put into words and a peace that will hold us together in the most stressful and darkest times of our lives. This doesn't mean we must wear a big grin on our faces and be unrealistic about our pain. Like Job, we should be honest, but it does mean that we can have complete confidence in knowing that God has triumphed over evil, and one day we will be pure gold!

3: Change your perspective – fix your eyes on Jesus

When driving along North Deeside Road heading to Aberdeen City, I see a church spire towering above the houses. From a distance, the spire appears to be on the right-hand side of the road, but as I follow the bend of the road and move closer to the church, I see that it is actually on the left-hand side. My perception – that is the way I saw and thought about the spire – changed the closer I got to it. To experience joy and peace in this world of pain, we need to change our perspective and move closer to God. **Let us fix our eyes on Jesus, the author and perfecter of our faith, who for the joy set before him endured the cross, scorning its shame, and sat down at the right hand of the throne of God.** (Hebrews 12:2) Jesus endured the cross by looking at **the joy set before him**, that is, the victory over sin and death. We are to follow His example and to **fix are our eyes on Jesus.** What does it mean to fix our eyes upon Him? It means we are to constantly be looking to Jesus for strength. We keep looking at Jesus. We don't look away. By fixing our gaze upon Him, we can endure suffering in this world.

Paul, who suffered much, was able to say, **I consider that our present sufferings are not worth comparing with the glory that will be revealed in us.** (Romans 8:18) Paul's perspective was Heavenward. He was able to view the pain in his life as something that would pass away when he entered into the presence of his Father. Through all Paul's hardships of imprisonment, torture, stoning, beatings, shipwrecks, rejection, and an unknown physical illness, he had complete peace and joy knowing Christ Jesus his King. He also knew that nothing in this world or the spiritual realm could separate him from the love of God, and nothing could cause him to lose this sure and certain hope. **For I am convinced that neither death nor life, neither angels nor demons, neither the present nor the future, nor any powers, neither height nor depth, nor anything else in all creation, will be able to separate us from the love of God that is in Christ Jesus our Lord.** (Romans 8:38-39)

The mind is a powerful influence upon our lives; what we think we often do, so we need to guard our thoughts and keep them holy. We live in an age of TV, DVDs, and the internet, where the potential for filling our minds with so much ungodly rubbish is very great. Christian men or women should not allow themselves to watch or read pornographic material or anything else that would spoil their friendship with God. We need to listen to His prompting through our conscience when we hear that quiet voice asking us, 'Is this honouring to God? Will it lead me away from Him?' we must respond. Paul understood the importance of having the right perspective and the need to train our minds heavenwards in order to experience God's peace. **...whatever is true, whatever is pure, whatever is right, whatever is admirable – if anything is excellent or praiseworthy – think about such things... And the God of peace will be with you.** (Philippians 4:8-9b)

The true Christian is like the pilgrims in John Bunyan's "Pilgrim's Progress". In this story, the Christian life is compared to a journey from this world to the next. Christian and his friends travel on foot from the City of Destruction to the celestial city. They meet many trials on their way, often make mistakes, but by the grace of God, they reach their destination. At one point, when they near the end of the journey, they see the celestial city from a distance, and the sight of it strikes them with homesickness because they long to be at home with their King. Many live as if God doesn't exist and are totally earthbound. (This is true even of Christians). **Their mind is on earthly things. But our citizenship is in heaven. And we eagerly await a Saviour from there, the Lord Jesus Christ, who, by the power that enables him to bring everything under his control, will transform our lowly bodies so that they will be like his glorious body.** (Philippians 3:19b-21) Are you and I focused upon our Lord Jesus? Do you eagerly await His return? Do you live in this world as someone passing through it, knowing that ultimately, we belong to Heaven? Do you and I live as citizens of Heaven – are you and I homesick? Someone once joked, 'He's so heavenly minded he's no earthly good.' But I want to challenge that and say it is those focused on Heaven, knowing life's purpose, who make any lasting difference to this world.

When Jesus says of His followers, **"You are the salt of the earth"** and **"You are the light of the world"**. (Matthew 5:13 & 14) He means that as salt adds flavour and prevents food from becoming putrid, so we can improve society and fight, even prevent, immorality and corruption. As light shows the way ahead, God's children are to show the way to Christ. While we live in this world, we are to be Christ-like and bear fruit, which affects other lives in positive ways.

I love the old-fashioned word, "behold". I think of John the Baptist, standing in the river Jordan, yelling at the top of his voice, **"Behold! The Lamb of God, who takes away the sin of the world!"** (John 1:29 ESVUK) Everyone who heard must have turned to the One he was pointing at and stared at Jesus. The word, "look", doesn't do justice to what is meant. To behold means more than to glance at something. It means to look and consider what you see and hear, to think about it, pause for a moment and take it in. I once visited the Laing Art Gallery, in Newcastle upon Tyne, and beheld a beautiful painting called, 'Isabella and the Pot of Basil' by William Holman Hunt. On seeing it, I was transfixed. I don't know how long I stood marvelling at it, how the artist had captured the skin tone, the complexities of hands and feet, the folds of the dress, and all the fine details of her surroundings, including the intricate patterns on the box that the pot of basil stood on. I got lost in the scene. I walked up as far as I was allowed to go to examine the brush strokes, and then I stood back to wonder at how thick blobs of paint were turned into a stunning, realistic portrait. I remembered that painting better than the ones I simply looked at for a moment. That is what it is to behold something.

<u>Let us change our perspective and behold the Lord Jesus.</u>

What do you see when you hear His name? What mental image do you have of Jesus? Few see a picture of a Jewish man with strong features, short hair, olive skin, and long sideburns that resemble tassels, but that's the image that comes to my mind. To most people, what comes to mind is a hippy-type, a man with long hair and a beard. Many picture Jesus as having long blond hair and blue eyes, which would have made Him stand out and merited comment by the gospel writers. I read a novel where Jesus was described as clean-shaven, reflecting the fact that early Roman mosaics portray Jesus as a man with short hair and no beard. To many religious people, the image that comes to mind is that of a crucifix – the emaciated broken body of a man hanging on a cross.

Any image we come up with, be it paintings, statues, or a mental image, is going to fall very short of the truth. Yes, Jesus was indeed crucified, but He did not stay on the cross – that is not where He is now – we relate to a risen Saviour now. We must try to avoid creating our own image of the Lord Jesus to ensure that we don't fall into the sin of idolatry.

When you read the four gospels, you are struck by the fact that there isn't a physical description of our Lord. (Except for the transfiguration; see below.) The writers, guided by the Holy Spirit, concentrated upon the person and character of Jesus and not on what He looked like. He must have appeared like any other young Jewish man of His time, for we read that people despised the carpenter from Nazareth who appeared so ordinary. Those from His hometown rejected Him because they couldn't see that Jesus was anything special. He was from a working-class family, not royalty; how could He claim to be the Messiah? There was nothing in His appearance to say that this Jesus from Nazareth was God in human flesh.

The Lord Jesus wore a veil over His glory, but on one occasion He lifted the veil so three of His disciples could glimpse His glory. **There he was transfigured before them. His face shone like the sun, and his clothes became as white as the light.** (Matthew 17:2) The time when Jesus' mortal appearance was transformed to reveal His awesome deity is only one of two physical descriptions given of Jesus in the entire New Testament. The other is in Revelation where the apostle John, now an old man and a prisoner because of his faith, sees the risen Lord:

I turned round to see the voice that was speaking to me. And when I turned, I saw seven golden lampstands, and among the lampstands was someone "like a son of man", dressed in a robe reaching down to his feet and with a golden sash round his chest. His head and hair were white like wool, as white as snow, and his eyes were like blazing fire. His feet were like bronze glowing in a furnace, and his voice was like the sound of rushing waters. In his right hand he held seven stars, and out of his mouth came a sharp double-edged sword. His face was like the sun shining in all its brilliance. When I saw him, I fell at his feet as though dead. Then he placed his

right hand on me and said: "Do not be afraid. I am the First and the Last. I am the Living One; I was dead, and behold I am alive for ever and ever! And I hold the keys of death and Hades." (Revelation 1:12-18)

I was meeting a friend for a time of prayer. Both of us had a busy week and were worn out. Both of us were feeling low in spirits. Talking together helped, but because I was going to speak on the above passage a few days later, I decided to read it before we prayed. Immediately my Christian brother and I felt our hearts strangely warmed. The fog that had descended within us was blown away by joy, and we had a great freedom in prayer. Our hearts were lighter and our problems insignificant because we had changed our perspective from ourselves to this amazing vision of the risen Saviour and King.

There is not enough space to give a detailed analysis of this passage. We cannot look at the symbolism in great depth, but we can consider a few of the brush strokes in this picture of the Lord Jesus. The title, the Son of Man, alludes to the name Jesus gave Himself to show that He was the fulfilment of the prophecy, in Daniel chapter seven, of the Messiah.

I continued watching in the night visions,

and I saw One like a son of man

coming with the clouds of heaven.

He approached the Ancient of Days

and was escorted before Him.

He was given authority to rule,

and glory, and a kingdom;

so that those of every people,

nation, and language

should serve Him.

His dominion is an everlasting dominion

that will not pass away,

and His kingdom is one

that will not be destroyed.

(Daniel 7:13-14 HCSB)

Messiah is the Jewish word for Christ, which comes from Greek. Both are titles, not names, meaning 'Anointed one'. They describe a man who has been set apart (made holy) by God to serve Him as a leader. Both priests and kings of Israel were anointed with oil to symbolise God's anointing with His Spirit. The way Jesus dressed reveals that He is the Messiah. He is clothed in the robe and sash of the High Priest and a king signifying His dual role as High Priest and King. He is the one who both offered the ultimate sacrifice and the one we are to obey.

His hair, **white like wool, as white as snow**, represents purity and Divine wisdom.

"As I kept watching, thrones were set in place,

and the Ancient of Days took His seat.

His clothing was white like snow,

and the hair of His head like whitest wool.

(Daniel 7:9 HCSB)

The most striking description is His eyes, which are like blazing fire. They reveal how penetrating Christ looks into our very souls; knows our every thought, and nothing is hidden from His sight. Eyes were considered to be windows of the soul, revealing the true character of a person, and thus the glory of God is unveiled. **Nothing in all creation is hidden from God's sight. Everything is uncovered and laid bare before the eyes of him, to whom we must give account.** (Hebrews 4:13)

His feet are like bronze glowing in a furnace. His feet stand out; they are made of metal; therefore this is a person of power. To be at a person's feet is a sign of respect. Being under a person's foot is a sign that they have power over us. **"Heaven is my throne, and the earth is my footstool."** (Acts 7:49) The bronze feet represent Jesus' absolute authority over all mankind and His victory over evil. **The God of peace will soon crush Satan under your feet.** (Romans 16:20) I also wonder if John mentions the feet because he saw where the nails had penetrated the heels of Jesus, and he recalled the prophecy in Genesis 3:15: **"...he will crush your head, and you will strike his heel."**

The mighty roar of His voice reveals the power of His word, so does the double-edged sword that comes out of His mouth. Jesus speaks to us words of comfort, encouragement, rebuke, and judgement. **For the word of God is living and active. Sharper than any double-edged sword, it penetrates even to dividing soul and spirit, joints and marrow; it judges the thoughts and attitudes of the heart.** (Hebrews 4:12) The words of the Lord Jesus to John are these: **"Do not be afraid. I am the First and**

the Last. I am the Living One; I was dead, and behold I am alive for ever and ever! And I hold the keys of death and Hades." He is the eternal God and the one who died in our place but is risen. He has conquered death itself and rules over the whole of the spiritual realm. So then, the true Christian isn't afraid of death; they have a different perspective. They are like John Bunyan, who pictured death, in the second part of Pilgrim's Progress, as an invitation from King Jesus to join Him in His eternal home.

We mustn't overlook the other things John sees, like the right hand of Jesus holding seven stars and the fact He stands among seven lampstands. We are told that the stars represent the seven angels of the seven churches John is writing to, and the lampstands symbolise the seven churches. Jesus is displaying His total power over the supernatural world and His absolute authority over the Church, not just those seven but the whole family of God.

The face of the Lord Jesus is amazing. The light emanating from within Him is so dazzling it is compared to the light of **the sun shining in all its brilliance** or full strength. Just pause and think for a moment: this light is so bright, not even the darkest of sunglasses would protect you from it! Here is displayed the glory of the Holy Son, who is the light of the world and God. **"I am the light of the world."** (John 9:4b) **God is light; in him there is no darkness at all.** (1 John 1:5b) **The light shines in the darkness, and the darkness has not overcome it.** (John 1:5)

The vision before John is so awesome that he struggles to describe what he sees, using lots of comparisons; this suggests that what John saw was even greater than what he

197

managed to put into words! This is the picture we need of the Lord Jesus. If Jesus appeared to us now, we would not be able to stand in His presence. Like John, our sense of our own sinfulness will cause us to fall at His feet in surrender and worship.

Focusing upon our Lord and what He has achieved for us produces great joy and peace. **You will keep in perfect peace all who trust in you, all whose thoughts are fixed on you!** (Isaiah 26:3 NLT)

The person who loves God will have a deep yearning to see Jesus face to face. The Bible promises that all true believers in Christ will be resurrected to eternal life and our bodies transformed to *be able to behold the face of glory*. Does the thought of seeing the One you love fill you with joy and give you peace? If that doesn't excite you, then you must question whether you have true faith at all. Do you long to have fellowship with Him without sin creeping into your heart and without any distractions whatsoever?

When we are in love, and we commit ourselves to another in marriage, the thought of our beloved husband or wife should bring a smile to our face as we experience the joy of being loved. Real love is devoted to the beloved. The Bible uses marriage to illustrate the relationship of God with His people, and the Church is called the bride of Christ. The very thought of God should bring joy to our hearts – no matter what our circumstances are – furthermore, we will be filled with a deep longing to see the object of our love. Now we can only glimpse His glory when we read the Bible; it's like looking in a mirror all misted up. **Now we see but a poor reflection as in a mirror; then**

we shall see face to face. Now I know in part; then I shall know fully, even as I am fully known. (1 Corinthians 13:12)

To experience joy and peace in this world of darkness, we need to cling to the promises of God, trust in the purpose of God, change our perspective onto God and finally, pray to God.

4: Pray to be filled with the Holy Spirit

The American evangelist, DL Moody, who lived in the 19th century, and whose preaching in Great Britain had a profound effect, was once asked why he prayed to be filled with the Holy Spirit every day; surely such a great man of God was already filled with Spirit? He replied simply, 'Because I leak!' When a person becomes a Christian, they are filled with the Holy Spirit – you can't be a Christian unless you've been made alive to God – but this filling is not a once-in-a-lifetime experience; it is a continuous event. The fact is we *do* leak, and that's a good thing. Jesus said: **"If anyone is thirsty, let him come to me and drink. Whoever believes in me, as the Scripture has said, streams of living water will flow from within him." By this he meant the Spirit, whom those who believed in him were later to receive.** (John 7:38-39a)

Think of a cup held under a tap of water. It fills up and overflows. And it keeps on filling up and overflowing. Now think of a cup held above other cups. As the cup overflows, it pours water into the others, and they too will overflow. The constant flow of water keeps the cups clean and the water pure. Don't think of a tap in a kitchen sink; think of an outside tap, where the water from the cups runs over into the garden, giving life to the plants. We are like cups, being filled and overflowing with the water of life to the benefit of all others. Out of the true believer will flow the evidence that God dwells within them. The fruit of the Spirit is visible proof that a person belongs to Christ. Being filled with the Spirit is a daily experience because it is the product of a friendship with God.

Praying is the language of our relationship with God. It is our doorway into the presence of our Father in Heaven. Praying keeps our relationship alive. **Come near to God and he will come near to you.** (James 4:8) It is all too easy to turn prayer into a lifeless ritual and part of religious duty, a thing we do in church or quickly for ten minutes a day. We can turn prayer into a chore, something we 'must do.' Prayer is often the last resort when all our plans have failed or we're in trouble. Praying can be difficult in this very busy world, with all its demands upon our time. Our own sinful natures get in the way of prayer, and our minds wander, or we become sleepy. The devil doesn't like us praying either, so he will hurl all sorts of distractions at us.

Those in full-time ministry, like pastors and missionaries, can fall into the trap of just praying as part of the job. I have to admit, in my early years as a London City Missionary, I did just that. I became so busy, I tended to pray or read the Bible only before giving a talk. Without realising it, my work as a missionary became more important than my friendship with God. Also, my work was becoming a tired routine, without any power or effect. Thankfully, other more mature missionaries gently put me right, and I protected my personal time reading the Bible and praying. I started reading the Bible for pleasure instead of studying it only to prepare a sermon or children's talk. I have forgotten how many times I have read the Bible because, following a wise colleague's advice, I read it cover to cover once every year. I read at a pace that suits me, and I pray that God will speak to me as I read.

Prayer is not a chore, or a duty, or a quick fix for our problems; it shouldn't be used as a last resort, for He should be the first person we consult when we have a difficult decision to make. **Do not be anxious about anything, but in everything, by prayer and petition, with thanksgiving, present your requests to God. And the peace of God, which transcends all understanding, will guard your hearts and your minds in Christ Jesus.** (Philippians 4:6-7)

Prayer is a pleasure, a privilege, a joy to the heart, a means of peace, and the more we pray, the greater and deeper our friendship with our Father becomes. Friends talk together. Prayer keeps the relationship alive. Sometimes our requests are not answered because if we had instant answers all the time, we'd never depend upon God and so miss out on knowing Him deeper.

We are encouraged to pray and keep on praying. Jesus taught about the need for persistence in prayer and for us to understand how much our Father loves us. **"Which of you fathers, if your son asks for a fish, will give him a snake instead? Or if he asks for an egg, will give him a scorpion? If you then, though you are evil, know how to give good gifts to your children,"** ... (The word evil here refers to the sinful nature and not any particular deed. Jesus was addressing ordinary, faithful Jews, who though sinful, were good fathers.) **"...how much more will your Father in heaven give the Holy Spirit to those who ask him!"** (Luke 11:11-13)

God will not withhold His Spirit from us, and so we can ask to be filled with the Spirit of God and to experience joy and peace. Be real in your prayers. God knows your thoughts, so don't try to hide them from Him. Tell Him as it is. Yes, He knows what you need before you ask, but He wants you to ask!

The psalms are wonderful examples of true faith pray-ers. Many were written in times of trial, and we can use them as the basis for our own prayers. Other prayers in the Bible are also helpful guides and good to pray. I remember feeling so low after having to leave my job due to ill health that I said to God, 'You have tossed me aside like an old slipper.' Later, I thought, 'What a terrible thing to say!' Then I read Psalm 102:10: **...you have taken me up and thrown me aside.** That psalmist felt the same as I did! By praying the prayer, I told God how I felt, and I learned that it wasn't true.

Our Father wants us to experience Him, and we need to wrestle in prayer, not just rattle off a 'God bless so and so today', but really engage with Him and not let Him go until He blesses us with His presence. He wants us to pour our hearts out, to praise Him, thank Him and enjoy Him. Ask for joy: **Restore to me the joy of your salvation...** (Psalm 51:12a) Jesus said, **"Peace I leave with you; my peace I give you."** (John 14:27) So, we can confidently ask for peace, trusting Him when He says: **"I tell you the truth, my Father will give you whatever you ask in my name... Ask and you will receive, and your joy will be complete."** (John 16:23-24)

Chapter Fifteen

Patiently waiting

But the fruit of the Spirit is...patience... (Galatians 5:22) I was once out for a walk with my son and my granddaughter, who was two at the time. My son is very tall, and when he walks, he takes long strides, making short time of any distance, but on this occasion, he took smaller steps, slowing down to match his little girl's pace. Our Heavenly Father does the same with us. He will walk *with* us at *our* pace. God will never hurry us to grow up too soon; He allows us to learn and is compassionate towards our failings; and will forgive us when we repent.

The LORD is merciful and gracious,

slow to anger and abounding in steadfast love.

(Psalm 103:8 ESVUK)

God patiently holding back judgement

Many of today's aggressive atheists try to assassinate God's loving character, taking passages in the Bible, about God's Holy and Just nature, out of context to prove their point. They present God as an angry, vengeful tyrant, just waiting for us to make mistakes so He can torment us. They will quote passages about Hell saying that only a cruel dictator would allow such a thing. As we have already seen, looking at God's justice and mercy, this is a false picture. The Father does *not* take pleasure in the death of the wicked, and that is why He gave us His Son, who descended into Hell on the cross so we could avoid that fate.

Another misconception is of God being a strict disciplinarian watching our every move, to pounce on us the moment we fail. Newly converted believers are prone to this wrong view of God (I know I was!) and have a carnal fear instead of true reverence. If a human father knows how to treat his children, how much more will our Father in Heaven know how to treat His children? Just as my son did not expect his toddler to take massive strides, so God remembers that we are frail human beings prone to falling down. Remember too that God doesn't keep a record of our wrongs – when He forgives, we remain forgiven.

... as far as the east is from the west,

so far has he removed our transgressions from us.

As a father has compassion on his children,

so the LORD has compassion on those who fear him;

for... he remembers that we are dust.

(Psalm 103:12-14)

Compassion is the demonstration of kindness. It is shown by action, by doing good to another and by giving someone time to admit their sins and turn from them. God gives us time to grow and to become holy. The process of being made holy takes a lifetime, and the more we take His hand when we stumble, the closer we get to the goal.

God's patience is not limited to true believers because He is incredibly patient with the whole of humanity. This explains why He has withheld His final judgement upon sin and evil. It is two thousand years since Christ ascended into Heaven, and we still await His promised return. The secular world mocks true faith for believing in the second coming of our Lord. **First of all, you must understand that in the last days scoffers will come, scoffing and following their own evil desires. They will say, "Where is this 'coming' he promised? Ever since our fathers died, everything goes on as it has since the beginning of creation."** (2 Peter 3:3-4) Have you wondered why it is taking so long for Jesus to return? Some false teachers say that the first Christians were mistaken when they took Christ's promise to be with us in the Spirit literally.

Others say that Jesus has already returned in a spiritual form. But the fact is that the Bible clearly teaches that the Lord will return physically and in such a way that the whole world will know about it. He will come, not as a humble baby but as the risen King that He is, in power and glory. But why, if He is to return to bring about the final defeat of evil and death, does He delay? The answer is pre-cisely because He is a compassionate God who does not delight in the death of the wicked. **The Lord is not slow in keeping his promise, as some understand slowness. He is patient with you, not wanting anyone to perish, but everyone to come to repentance.** (2 Peter 3:9)

In Luke chapter 15, Jesus compared God to a loving fa-ther who waits for his disobedient son to return to him. The son, who has wasted his father's wealth on wild living and who realises his wretched state, returns to the family home to beg for the position of a servant. In the distance, he sees his father, tossing all dignity aside and running down the path to meet him. Instead of punishment, he is shown mercy and is restored to the family, not as a slave but as a rightful heir. God longs for His creation to repent. He waits for us to come to Him. His word still speaks: **...now is the time of God's favour, now is the day of salvation.** (2 Co-rinthians 6:2b) Out of patient love, God holds back the time of His Son's return and the final day of judgement.

Patiently waiting for His return

This knowledge should create a holy dilemma in the hearts of all true Christians. We should be longing for Christ's return, praying earnestly, '**Come Lord Jesus.**' (Revelation 22:20b) and at the same time, we should be praying, 'Have mercy O Lord, be patient, wait for more people to come to you! O Lord, revive your Church, pour out your Spirit, turn the tide of evil and bring a time of renewal where You are at the centre of my community and country.'

Does that describe you? Do you pray for family, friends, neighbours, and even your enemies to come to Christ and be made right with God? When was the last time you asked God for a revival? Do you long for a time when God is at the centre of your community, when every Christian, including yourself, is living exactly as they should be? Do you pray for a time when there is no doubt about the power of God and, as a result, many forsake evil? There have been revivals in the past, changing lives so dramatically that the local police were not needed, and it can happen again. We need to keep crying out … **your kingdom come, your will be done on earth as it is in heaven.** (Matthew 6:10)

Even though God is patient, He will send His Son back – we don't know when that will be – it will come upon the world when it least expects it. **But the day of the Lord will come like a thief. The heavens will disappear with a roar; the elements will be destroyed by fire, and the earth and everything in it will be laid bare. Since everything will be destroyed in this way, what kind of people ought you to be? You ought to live holy and godly lives as you look forward to the day of God and speed its coming. That day will bring about the destruction of the heavens by fire, and the elements will melt in the heat.** (2 Peter 3:10-12)

Living holy and godly lives, being what God intends us to be, and declaring the message of salvation to the world, will speed His return. But if His return means judgement, why would we want to speed it up? The answer is that judgement against evil and injustice is a good thing – it means the end of evil and suffering however, judgement is only one aspect of His return: **But in keeping with his promise, we are looking forward to a new heaven and a new earth, the home of righteousness. So then, dear friends, since you are looking forward to this, make every effort to be found spotless, blameless, and at peace with him.** (2 Peter 3:13-14) **Be patient, then, brothers, until the Lord's coming.** (James 5:7)

In John Bunyan's *Pilgrim's Progress,* Christian witnesses an acted parable when he meets two boys called Passion and Patience. Passion is restless, bored with life, while Patience is content. A huge bag of treasure is laid at the feet of Passion. He has all the things this world offers. He is overjoyed and sets about to spend, play, and use up the treasure, but it soon goes, and his toys are broken. All his hopes and dreams lie scattered at his feet, and he ends up in rags with nothing good to look forward to. Meanwhile, Patience remains content and full of hope because his treasure is in Heaven. He is looking forward to the rewards in the life to come; he is not living for this life and the things the world offers but for his God, trusting that He will provide what he needs.

I find it heart-breaking that we Christians can argue over the details of the Lord's return and waste time in trying to work out how and when God will fulfil His promises. The simple fact is – we don't know: **"No-one knows about that day or hour, not even the angels in heaven, nor the Son, but only the Father."** (Matthew 24:36) Even Jesus, while He was in His humbled state, did not know when He would return. The teaching of the Bible is clear that the Lord will return; we don't know when, so we must be ready. We get ready by being holy – set apart for God – living the life He has given us and producing the fruit of the Holy Spirit. We are to witness to the world by remembering that we are citizens of Heaven and not living for this world's passing pleasures, which results in impatience.

What causes fights and quarrels among you? Don't they come from your desires that battle within you? You want something but don't get it. (James 4:1-2a) Would you like to have a content and happy heart? Then be patient and don't strive for material things. Imitate Paul, who could say: **I know what it is to be in need, and I know what it is to have plenty. I have learned the secret of being content in any and every situation, whether well fed or hungry, whether living in plenty or in want. I can do everything through him who gives me strength.** (Philippians 4:12-13)

Paul's focus was upon Christ. Knowing God was the most important thing in his life, and as a result, he didn't let times of plenty go to his head. Paul didn't make an idol of material possessions – he could live without them – so when in need, he was still content. God gave Paul the strength to endure hardship and have the right attitude to worldly things when life was running smoothly.

It may surprise 21st century Christians, living in an increasingly secular society, that in Victorian times and the early part of the 20th century, a person gained great respect from society if they were members of the church, especially the Church of England. Many professed faith in God and had a veneer of respectability as a means of getting on in business. Read the books of Charles Dickens, and you'll see this hypocrisy in a number of his characters. Gaining respect through religion is nothing new as we see in Paul's condemnation of those **... of a corrupt mind, who have been robbed of the truth and who think that godliness is a means to financial gain.** (1 Timothy 6:5)

This error has presented itself in a different form in modern times by those who preach a Prosperity Gospel. This teaching says that when you are right with God, filled with His Spirit, He will bless you (which is true) but, the blessings take the form of material wealth, good jobs, re-spect from society, and healthy bodies (which isn't true). The problem with this view – that Christians have a right to health and wealth – is that it is contrary to the teaching of God's word, and it's unrealistic. Many have been put off Christianity by telly evangelists constantly asking for money and clearly lining their own pockets.

Paul shows that godliness can actually mean hatred and persecution from the world. **In fact, everyone who wants to live a godly life in Christ Jesus will be persecuted...** (2 Timothy 3:12) True godliness, being like Christ, results in opposition from the world. We do not use our faith in God for gaining what we want in this life.

Christians in wealthy countries often struggle to have a correct attitude towards material things, and it's difficult in a consumer society where we are bombarded with adverts. The young are particularly vulnerable, with the pressure from peers, the media, and advertisers to conform and get the latest gadget or fashion item. One extreme is that we can possess as much as we want to. The other is to deny ourselves and others any material possessions except basic food and clothing. There are folk who say we should not watch television, let alone own a set or a computer. They forbid attending dances, cinemas, and dining out. Some withdraw from society altogether and become monks, nuns, or hermits.

So, these are the two extremes: expect heath and wealth or live without anything that gives pleasure. It is a question of balance. We may be heading for Heaven, but in the meantime, we live in this world and need certain things which God provides. The danger comes when we live for the things in this world instead of living for God. Like Bunyan's pilgrim, we need to remember that we are passing through this world towards one that is far better and not let ourselves be distracted from our purpose in life.

I write as someone who hasn't always got the balance right, but the question to ask yourself is; 'I am truly content with what I have and trust God to provide, or have I given in to the sin of covetousness – just wanting things for the sake of wanting? If I were to lose everything overnight, would I still praise God or would I criticise Him? Would my world have ended, or can I say, 'Jesus is my world?''

We need to ... **fix our eyes not on what is seen, but on what is unseen. For what is seen is temporary, but what is unseen is eternal.** (2 Corinthians 4:18)

But godliness with contentment is great gain. For we brought nothing into the world, and we can take nothing out of it. But if we have food and clothing, we will be content with that. People who want to get rich fall into temptation and a trap and into many foolish and

harmful desires that plunge men into ruin and destruction. For the love of money is a root of all kinds of evil. Some people, eager for money have wandered from the faith and pierced themselves with many griefs. (1 Timothy 6:5-10) These words surely contain a warning about gambling. A child of God should trust their Father to provide what they need and not the randomness of a lottery or a racetrack. May God give us the grace to be content with what we have and in all circumstances.

Jesus didn't condemn the rich for having lots of money; He condemned them for making riches the goal of their lives. **"What good is it for a man to gain the whole world, yet forfeit his soul?"** (Mark 8:36) Paul wasn't condemning the rich Christians either but cautioning them not to rely upon their riches. **Command those who are rich in this present world not to be arrogant nor to put their hope in wealth, which is so uncertain, but to put their hope in God, who richly provides us with everything for our enjoyment. Command them to do good, to be rich in good deeds, and to be generous and willing to share. In this way they will lay up treasure for themselves as a firm foundation for the coming age, so that they may take hold of the life that is truly life.** (1 Timothy 6:17-19)

Jesus said: **"But store up for yourselves treasures in heaven, where moth and rust do not destroy, and where thieves do not break in and steal. For where your treasure is, there your heart will be also."** (Matthew 6:20, 21) Without a doubt, the treasure is God Himself and the exquisite pleasure of seeing Him face to face, but I think it is also the joy of seeing those we have prayed for in glory with us.

Practising patience through prayer and personal witness

While we wait for His return, the Lord expects us to make new disciples. When Jesus ascended into Heaven, the apostles stared up at the sky longingly. Two angels suddenly appeared and said, **"Men of Galilee, why do you stand here looking into the sky? This same Jesus, who has been taken from you into heaven, will come back in the same way you have seen him go into heaven."** (Acts 1:11) The Apostles returned to Jerusalem and obeyed Christ's last instruction to them. They were not to be passively waiting for the Lord to return but were to actively tell others of His resurrection and demonstrate His love in practical ways, which is what they did. Patiently waiting doesn't mean that we idly stare up at the clouds but that we make the most of every opportunity to display perfect love.

What are you like when you are waiting for something? What's your mood in a traffic jam – are you nice and calm? How patient are you waiting to see the doctor or standing in a queue? Do you mutter under your breath, 'Oh come on!'? None of us are particularly good when we have to wait. We need to see these times of waiting as opportunities to pray. Modern life is hectic, and these times when all we can do is wait are opportunities to use our time for silent prayer. Instead of getting irritable with the cars in front, pray for the people in the cars. Pray for those in the queue, say hello to them instead of ignoring them; you never know if God is giving you an opportunity to share your faith unless you try. Instead of being frustrated with the busy doctor, pray for him or her. Do you get impatient with the present government? Pray for them!

The London Underground is an amazing place. Hundreds of people crammed into a small carriage rattling along a dark tunnel; people nose to nose with each other and not one person speaking to the other. It's fascinating to watch a mass of humanity all in one place, all locked into their own little worlds via earphones plugged into music devices, or phones, books, or simply staring out into the blackness, just waiting for the train to reach its destination with no concern for the person next to them. That's not how Christians should live, simply waiting for the end, never reaching out to those we rub noses with. We have a message – a great message – that enables them to reach their final destination, and we dare not keep it to ourselves, so while we wait, we must reflect our Father in Heaven. God hears our silent prayers and blesses those times of forced waiting by giving us peace in place of frustration.

<u>Practising patience with fellow believers</u>

It is very easy to forget that our fellow believers struggle with sin as we do. Sometimes we expect too much, too soon from our brothers and sisters in Christ, especially pastors and teachers whom we regard as spotless saints. There is a tendency to forget that men of God, who faithfully preach the gospel, are also frail human beings subject to fierce temptations from Satan. This partly explains our shock when a Church leader confesses adultery.

216

Do you regularly pray for your pastors and leaders? Do you pray that they will be grounded in God's word, filled with His Spirit, and given wisdom? Do you pray for their daily walk and their protection from giving in to temptation? Remember that it's not only sexual temptations but subtle sins such as pride, overconfidence, neglecting personal devotions due to busy schedules; a desire to be relevant by keeping up with the times, leading to compromise with sinful world values and a lack of patience with members of the church or their own family.

Beware of becoming critical and falling into the sin of gossiping, especially about those who serve in some leadership role. Instead of criticising the leadership for taking their time over something, pray that God will give them the wisdom to know His will on the matter and for the resources to carry out His work. All believers are torn between two worlds. There is a desire to be with God in Heaven, but meanwhile, we serve Him in this fallen world, where sin is still a powerful influence.

I remember a poster that said: 'Be patient with me; God hasn't finished with me yet!' It is good for us to be aware that we, and our fellow believers, are not yet perfect. Instead of impatience **... let us consider how we may spur one another on towards love and good deeds. Let us not give up meeting together, as some are in the habit of doing, but let us encourage one another – and all the more as you see the Day approaching.** (Hebrews 10:24-25)

Practical patience

The letter of James is very practical and gives us a clear guide on how we can exercise patience. **Everyone should be quick to listen, slow to speak and slow to become angry...** (James 1:19)

Quick to listen: Patience will wait and truly listen to another person. We should take the trouble to concentrate upon the words being spoken to us and understand them. So many arguments result from misunderstandings due to not properly hearing what has been said. A good listener is sometimes all the medicine a stressed person needs.

Slow to speak: I have a particular failing when excited and in conversation. My mind works quickly, and I'm itching to express my thoughts before the other person has finished speaking just in case I forget what I want to say. However, I hate it when someone interrupts *me* when I'm speaking! Conversation has been called an art. I'm not sure about that, but I am sure it's an exercise in patience. How often have you regretted something you've said? The mother's advice to think before you speak is sound. Patience waits and weighs up words before speaking them. Once a word is out of your mouth, it is impossible to put it back.

Our daily prayer should be the same as the psalmist; **Set a guard over my mouth, O LORD; keep watch over the door of my lips.** (Psalm 141:3) When I was a child, I used to mouth the words of a silly rhyme: 'Sticks and stones will break my bones, but names (or words) will never hurt me.' Even as I said it, I knew it was a lie to try and soften the blow of being called a nasty name. Words are powerful.

64They can wound, and they can heal. They can start a war or end one. **With the tongue we praise our Lord and Father, and with it we curse men, who have been made in God's likeness. Out of the same mouth comes praise and cursing. My brothers, this should not be.** (James 3:9-10)

<u>Slow to become angry</u>: It is interesting that James does not tell his readers not to be angry but to be *slow* to become angry. As we have already seen, there is righteous anger – the anger directed at wrong and evil deeds. Righteous anger requires self-control to avoid it becoming sinful rage. Patience will be slow to anger, just as our Father is slow to become angry and ready to forgive. Impatience leads me to take offence easily. We live in a society that encourages folk to 'stand on their rights.' People become extremely angry when they feel that their 'rights' have been infringed. I find it fascinating how those who shout, 'I know my rights', never consider the rights of the person they are angry at.

A child of God should not behave in this way. If we have been to the foot of the cross, then we will know that we have no rights at all and be eternally thankful for the mercy shown to us. The works of the sinful nature include **fits of rage... but the fruit of the Spirit is ...patience.** (Galatians 5:20, 22) We show patience to someone else is by remembering to put into practice the 'golden rule' **... in everything, do to others what you would have them do to you...** (Matthew 7:12) Put yourself in the other person's place and think how you would feel if they treated you unjustly. A quick temper should have no place in the heart of a Christian, **for man's anger does not bring about the righteous life that God desires.** (James 1:19 - 20) You may be thinking, 'This is easier said than done. I ask for patience but still don't have it.' Perhaps you are asking for the wrong thing. Don't ask for patience; ask for power. We need to ask for the power of God to enable us to produce this fruit of the Spirit.

'When we ask God for power, we normally think of healing or some dramatic manifestation. But Paul asks for power **for all endurance and patience, with joy** (Colossians 1:11 HCSB). God gives us power to persevere, perhaps in suffering or facing great opposition. He empowers us to be patient, perhaps with depressing work scenarios or ageing parents, and He empowers us to have a joyful spirit in our struggles, like Paul and Silas singing in prison. We love the dramatic and eye-catching, but perhaps we need to ask for power to grow in godliness a little more.' Dr Jeremy McQuoid

Learning patience in affliction

I have already spoken at length about suffering, but there is one aspect I did not touch on, and that was how God uses suffering as a teacher. A car must be able to do what it was built for, and it must be able to withstand some pretty tough conditions. The manufacturer will test a car by putting it in a wind tunnel, subjecting it to extremes in heat and cold; the tests used for a car are designed to reveal the car's strengths and weaknesses. God will allow tough times for the same reason, with the difference that He will stand in the wind tunnel with us.

Times of affliction reveal how real our faith in God is and our reaction to stress shows us what is within our hearts. It can be a sober moment when you realise that you snapped under stress, and you said something you shouldn't have. Affliction can reveal how real our faith is, whether you have a sunshine faith or one for all seasons. Those with a genuine trust in God will persevere and learn patience as they wait upon God.

Consider it pure joy... whenever you face trials of many kinds, because you know that the testing of your faith produces perseverance. Let perseverance finish its work so that you may be mature and complete, not lacking anything. (James 1:2-4) **You have heard of Job's perseverance and have seen what the Lord finally brought about. The Lord is full of compassion and mercy.** (James 5:11)

Raw suffering, intense pain and loss make us revaluate what is important in life. We give up those sins that have been revealed through the stress. We learn how to treat others better, and we are less likely to fly off in a fit of rage. Suffering shows us how limited our resources are when we come to the end of ourselves. When we are in a situation where there is nothing we can do to make things better – and no-one else can help us – we discover that God is holding on to us. He uses suffering to make us into gold – pure and perfect in His sight. Patience means I am more dependent upon my Father in Heaven than anyone else, and I learn that He has used the pain to mould me in to His image.

I am not very good at waiting; I would like things to happen far more quickly than they do, and I think that is true of all of us. One way that God is teaching me to wait and be patient is to put me in situations where waiting on Him is the only option. I have marvelled at how He has fought the battle for me many times and how events have turned out in a way I did not expect. The faithful servants of God in the Old Testament learned that God can do the unexpected. Joshua defeated the fortress city of Jericho when he relied upon the LORD to fight the battle. David slew Goliath, declaring that the battle belonged to God.

Jehoshaphat's godliness was revealed when three countries threatened Judah. His kingdom and resources were small and weak, but on hearing the reports of a vast army approaching, Jehoshaphat proclaimed a fast for all Judah and called everyone to a prayer meeting. Just imagine that happening today! Asking the God and Father of our Lord Jesus Christ for help would not be on the top of the list of national leaders, and even believers can be slow to call a prayer meeting in a time of crisis. For this godly king, prayer came first. He knew his limitations and trusted in the LORD God completely. How many leaders today would pray, **"We do not know what to do, but our eyes are upon you."**? (2 Chronicles 20:12b)

God answered them. **'Do not be afraid or discouraged because of this vast army. For the battle is not yours, but God's. Tomorrow march down against them... You will not have to fight the battle... stand firm and see the deliverance the LORD will give you, O Judah and Jerusalem. Do not be afraid; do not be discouraged... the LORD will be with you.'** (2 Chronicles 20:15-17)

The response of the king, and the people, was to wor-ship God and take Him at His word, so much so that the army marched to the battleground proceeded by a choir! They praised God before they saw the outcome because they *knew* that He would fight the battle. **As they began to sing and praise, the LORD set ambushes against the men of Ammon and Moab and Mount Seir who were invading Judah, and they were defeated. The men of Ammon and Moab rose up against the men from Mount Seir to destroy and annihilate them. After they finished slaughtering the men from Seir, they helped to destroy one another.** (2 Chronicles 20:22-23) God turned their evil upon their own heads. We are not told how they became confused, but that is what happened. The three armies at-tacked each other, believing that the opposition was Judah, and they were so bloodthirsty they carried on until they were all destroyed.

Are you in a no-win situation, where, whatever you do or say can be used against you? You are helpless, and you don't know what to do. Wait upon God. Exercise patience just like Jehoshaphat and Judah, who were content in knowing that God would fight the battle for them. It is im-portant to note that Jehoshaphat and his people were not passive; they didn't fold their arms waiting for God – they obeyed Him. They gave Him the first place of honour in their lives, and they put their faith into practice by doing what He told them to do. God would have us carry on living godly lives, doing what is right, living to His standards, demonstrating His love and goodness in the face of adver-sity, and not returning evil for evil.

'Trust and obey, for there's no other way
To be happy in Jesus,
But to trust and obey.'
(John Henry Sammis 1848-1919)

Whatever the situation you face – only you know what it is – no matter how impossible it seems, let God fight the battle for you and: **Be joyful in hope, patient in affliction, faithful in prayer.** (Romans 12:12) We are not to be joyful for the crisis but to have joy in the hope founded upon God. Hope is shown by patiently waiting upon Him and persisting in prayer. Those who waited upon God in the Bible were never disappointed.

Patient with the afflictions of others

When God has answered our prayers in a way we never imagined, and the crisis is over, we can respond in one of three ways. First, we forget and pretend that nothing has happened and carry on as before. Second, we wallow in the memories of the pain, forever going over the same things, talking to others about it, and never moving on. Third, we learn from the experience and use it to help others in similar circumstances. This third response is the Biblical one, as suffering should give me empathy with those who suffer, leading me to demonstrate a compassionate patience.

Sin will make us impatient with other people (and ourselves), especially when a difficult situation drags on. People in trauma can be very demanding of our time and energy. Those with mental or emotional issues can really test our patience. We might be tempted to tell them to pull themselves together, stop moaning or such like, but if we have been in the darkness and someone's patient kindness was a light to us, then surely we ought to apply the grace we have received to those who come to us for help. God is **the Father of compassion and the God of all comfort, who comforts us in all our troubles, so that we can comfort those in any trouble with the comfort we ourselves have received from God.** (2 Corinthians 1:3-4)

Patient kindness is sometimes all a person needs, especially from fellow believers. The friends of Job acted wisely when they simply sat with him, weeping and saying nothing for seven days. The problems came when they opened their mouths and judged the casualty. I have found that one of the most painful things in life is watching a person you love go through suffering. It is during these times we need the patience of our Lord Jesus. I have met folk who feel guilty because they almost wished that a loved one would hurry up and die. Watching a loved one suffer creates powerful and draining emotions that confuse us.

The truth is that we do not want that person to die – we want the pain to end – but sometimes, we know that death is inevitable, so we can become impatient, not with the person, but with the *pain* and whatever is causing it. Wanting the suffering to stop is not wrong, so be patient with yourself and let the patience of our God and Father flow out of you towards the loved one. Remember that He understands your confusion and pain. Hold onto this promise: **The eternal God is your refuge, and underneath are the everlasting arms.** (Deuteronomy 33:27) Isn't that simply a wonderful picture of the Heavenly Father! He's a refuge in the storms of life; His loving arms are supporting us in the pain. It suggests to my mind a celestial hug! He will never let go of you, He is the Shepherd who knows each one of His sheep by name, and no-one and nothing can snatch His loved ones from His hand. Patience equals trust. Trust in Christ receives an eternal reward.

Chapter Sixteen

The Kind, Good and

Faithful Mirror

But the fruit of the Spirit is...kindness, goodness, faithfulness... (Galatians 5:22) I have taken these three aspects of the fruit of the Spirit together because, in many ways, we have already touched upon them in other chapters. Indeed, it is difficult to separate these qualities because they are one fruit, all being aspects of the love of God that true Christians reflect.

<u>Kindness</u>

Love is patient, love is kind. (1 Corinthians 13:4) Kindness is love in action. It is love demonstrated by compassion. Jesus revealed God's kindness in His earthly life. The Gospels portray a man full of compassion for the lost and outcasts of society. He changed the lives of prostitutes, thieves, beggars, lepers; the rich, the poor, the young, and the old. Jesus broke down racial and social barriers. He reached out to His own people, the Jews, while ignoring the prejudices of the times by welcoming Samaritans, Greeks, and the despised Romans.

The kindness of Jesus is demonstrated by His miracles of healing which were motivated by compassion. Compassion is a deep sense of empathy, moved to action. Jesus didn't simply talk about love – He showed it. He didn't just feel sorry for someone in need He did something about it. A centurion, who was a Roman soldier in command of a hundred men, sent a message to Jesus asking Him to come and heal His servant. Later, He came with another message displaying complete faith in Jesus by telling Him that He didn't have to attend to the patient in person, all He had to do was give the word, and the servant would be healed. After commending the man's deep faith, Jesus heals the servant with a word. The Lord healed a low servant – possibly a slave – and a servant of a Roman! His act of kindness led to the salvation of the centurion's household. The story is related in Matthew 8 and Luke 7, chapters that display other examples of the kindness of the King of Kings.

Another example of Jesus' kindness is found on the night He was arrested. Jesus is seized by a mob sent from the high priest. **Then Simon Peter, who had a sword, drew it and struck the high priest's servant, cutting off his right ear.** (John 18:10) **But Jesus answered, "No more of this!" And he touched the man's ear and healed him.** (Luke 22:51) Notice once again this is a person considered to be nothing much; someone at the beck and call of another – owned by the man who wanted Jesus dead –

but our Lord does not allow Himself to be led away until He heals the man. Jesus did not think of Himself even at that moment of danger, instead, He put His own needs aside in favour of another human being.

Kind words and kind deeds flowed out of Jesus like a pure river in flood. Those who are like Him show kindness. They do so with their thoughts: thinking others to be better than themselves. They do so with their words: never saying anything to crush a person's spirit but only words that will build up another. They do so with their actions: being the first to serve others and lend a helping hand. **Do nothing out of selfish ambition or vain conceit, but in humility consider others better than yourselves. Each of you should look not only to your own interests, but also to the interests of others. Your attitude should be the same as that of Christ Jesus...** (Philippians 2:3-5)

Kindness to the poor is a loan to the LORD, and He will give a reward to the lender. (Proverbs 19:17 HCSB) This is similar to: **I tell you the truth, whatever you did for one of the least of these brothers of mine, you did for me.** (Matthew 25:40) Giving kindness is the Christian's act of worship to God; we demonstrate our love for Him when we show it to others.

Goodness

Good and goodness are overused words. We describe many things as being good. We say, 'the food is good', meaning that it tastes delicious and nourishes us, but is it good in the Biblical sense of the word? We talk about seeing a 'good'

film or play, meaning that it was well made, kept our interest, entertained us, and told us an engaging story. But was
the film or play truly good? Many plays and films contain
things that are offensive to a holy God. 'That is a good
book,' we say, meaning that it was written well, held our
attention, entertained us, and made us think. The Bible used
to be referred to as, 'the Good Book', so is every book good
in the same way? We describe inanimate objects like cars
as being good and what we mean is the car was designed
well, built to a high standard, runs efficiently, and is easy
to drive but can an inanimate object really be good?

The word 'good' is applied to so many things it has lost
its true meaning. Jesus challenged a rich man for using the
word without grasping its true significance. **"Why do you
call me good?" Jesus answered. "No-one is good – except God alone."** (Mark 10:18) Jesus was challenging the
man's perception of goodness and the casual way he used
the word. In effect, Jesus was saying something like, 'Why
give Me a title that belongs to God? God alone is good. If
you call Me good, then you must believe I am God.' Jesus
defines goodness as being God's nature. We have seen that
one of the characteristics of God is holiness – God *is* good!
He is pure and morally perfect, with absolutely no defect
and no trace of evil. If we call Jesus good, then we are declaring Him to be God.

We are urged in the Bible to lead holy lives. Lives set
apart from all that is opposed to God. Goodness is the mark
that the believer is like their King Jesus. Goodness is the
mirror becoming bright, reflecting the Holy One within the
heart. The secular world rejects God. But the true Christian

loves God and shows this by having a real friendship with Him.

Hate what is evil; cling to what is good... Do not be overcome by evil, but overcome evil with good. (Romans 12:9 & 21) **For you were once darkness, but now you are light in the Lord. Live as children of light (for the fruit of the light consists in all goodness, righteousness and truth) and find out what pleases the Lord.** (Ephesians 5:8-10)

Many people do good things like giving to charity or devoting their lives to helping those in need. But not everyone's good deed can be described in the Biblical definition of the word "good". Genuine goodness results from a relationship with Christ; it is not separate from Him but displayed by His Spirit within us. [He] **gave himself for us to redeem us** (set us free) **from all wickedness and to purify for himself a people that are his very own, eager to do what is good.** (Titus 2:14) Goodness is the mark of being the people belonging to Christ. **"You are the light of the world... let your light shine before men, that they may see your good deeds and praise your Father in heaven.** (Matthew 5:14 & 16)

As children of God, we must not be shy of showing goodness. "A good deed" is the outworking of God's very own goodness and will point others to Him. I am not good in and of myself. Compared to God, no human being can be described as good because God is utterly set apart from sin. To say that a person is good is to say that you see something of God within them. The only good within me is what

God has put there. I am only truly good and do good things when I obey Him and live like my King Jesus.

The Holy Spirit produces goodness within us – goodness that is seen. In other words, we are made *saints*. The New Testament calls Christians *saints* – all Christians, not just a few. **To all in Rome who are loved by God and called to be saints...** (Romans 1:7) **To the saints in Ephesus...** (Ephesians 1:1b) **To all the saints in Christ Jesus at Philippi....** (Philippians 1:1b) There are many other references and not just in the New Testament. All true believers in Christ are saints.

The dictionary defines a saint as someone who has been honoured by the church after they have died, or someone exceptional and chosen by God because of their righteousness. Both these definitions are not the way the Bible uses the word. During the time this book was written, the Roman Catholic Church decided to make Pope John Paul II and Mother Teresa of Calcutta into saints. According to the church, the deceased pontiff and the nun had worked miracles. The claims were tested, and then they were canonised; that is, they were both made into a saint. This is not the Biblical teaching; God makes saints, not man. A saint is a person God has changed and is changing. He alone makes a person righteous. A saint is not some extraordinary person who has done an unusual thing. Every true believing Christian is a saint. If you are in Christ Jesus, *you* are a saint! The words saint and holy have the same root word in the original language. To be a saint means to be holy. Paul addresses the Corinthian believers as saints but uses a different form of words: **.... to those sanctified in Christ Jesus and called to be holy...** (1 Corinthians 1:2) That word, sanctified, means to be made a saint or set apart, which is the meaning of the word holy.

Goodness or holiness is the mark of a Spirit-filled Christian. I like the definition Martyn Lloyd-Jones gave of the word holy: '... that we are separated from everything that separates us *from* God.' So a saint is separated from the secular world that hates God. But Lloyd-Jones' definition doesn't stop at the negative. It is not enough that I distance myself from the thinking of the sinful world and its behaviour because that simply makes me a moral man, but not a holy man. 'The thing that makes us saints is that we are separated *to God.* Not only from the world but to God in particular; and that we are concerned about the glory of God and that we give ourselves to the service of God.' The proof that we are Christ's is that we will be good – not just moral, upright people – but *God's* people, with *His* goodness pouring out of us to His glory and praise.

Faithfulness

Faithfulness is loyalty flowing from faith. Faith is dependence and trust. The person who trusts God completely will also be faithful to Him. Christians will be like their Lord in this respect as He was totally dedicated to His Father and faithfully carried out His Father's will. Fear of offending the Holy One keeps the Christian from committing wilful sins. When you love God, He will be of first importance to you and so you will be faithful to His commands. Loving God means doing one's best to avoid offending Him in any way. This means that a Christian should be a faithful employer, caring for their staff, and a faithful employee, working hard at a given task. The believer should be a faithful husband or wife, and a faithful child, avoiding anything that dishonours the family.

It was fear of offending God that prevented Joseph from committing adultery. Joseph, the son of Israel, remembered his father and his father's God when he was taken off to live as a slave in Egypt. Joseph was away from his father's influence but had not forgotten what his father had taught him about God. Even more importantly, Joseph had his own faith, and this was displayed by his complete loyalty. When the wife of his Egyptian master tempted Joseph to have sex with her, he declared that he had the trust of his master, who had given everything in the household to his charge. **"My master has withheld nothing from me except you because you are his wife. How then could I do such a wicked thing and sin against God?" And though she spoke to Joseph, day after day, he refused to go to bed with her or even to be with her.** (Genesis 39:9-10)

There is much to learn from Joseph. He was loyal firstly to God, and then this led to loyalty to his master. Yes, Joseph was a slave, but he did his best for his master and earned his respect and trust. Joseph would not betray that trust. The thought of stealing his master's wife was repugnant. His motive for refusing her advances was fear and love for God. He knew that ultimately he would be disobeying God. This is interesting because this was long before the Law of Moses was given, so Joseph revealed that the law of God was written on his heart.

To resist the temptation, Joseph not only refused to listen to her but also avoided her company. Wise man that he was; he did not put himself in a situation where he could be enticed by sin. The wife laid a careful trap, sending all the other slaves out of the house and waiting for Joseph to attend to his duties. She tried again, but Joseph literally ran away from her. His faithfulness to God and his master cost Joseph his freedom because the wife falsely accused Joseph of raping her, and the husband believed her lie. Even in the dungeon, Joseph remained faithful and worked hard, gaining the respect and trust of the jailer. The account ends with Joseph being rewarded for his faithfulness and being made the Prime Minister of Egypt; you can read the story in Genesis 39-41.

Christians, in countries with oppressive regimes, are losing their freedom and lives because of their faithfulness to Christ. The number of persecuted believers is an ever growing number. How faithful we will be, if and when we face persecution, depends on the place we give to Christ now. We remain faithful by keeping our eyes upon our Lord Jesus. The Christian who loves God above all will also love those He gives to them, and this love for God and your spouse keeps you faithful. Like Joseph, we should treat sin and temptation – in all its shapes and forms – like a raging bull and run away from it.

Sin is subtle, so be careful with the man or woman you work with. Your friendship may be perfectly correct but beware of Satan's craftiness. You may find yourself working with that person a lot on a particular project. You may have to meet to discuss an important point over a coffee, and gradually the enemy of souls entices you, so you develop feelings for that person, or you find you have a lot in common and then before you realise it, you are having an affair with your colleague. I could have easily given the example of two committed Christians working together for the church. Many good men and women have fallen because they did not run away at the first hint of temptation. **Flee from sexual immorality.** (1 Corinthians 6:18) **Flee the evil desires of youth, and pursue righteousness, faith, love and peace, along with those who call on the Lord out of a pure heart.** (2 Timothy 2:22) We need to pray and keep alert, watching out for subtle signs of temptation.

We need to ask God for a very sensitive conscience. We must hear God's alarm bells before the fire breaks out and consumes us. **Be self-controlled and alert. Your enemy the devil prowls around like a roaring lion looking for someone to devour. Resist him, standing firm in the faith...** (1 Peter 5:8-9a)

How do we avoid sexual sins? Indeed, how do we avoid any form of sin? As we have seen, we need to walk in step with the Holy Spirit. We need to keep our relationship with Jesus alive and abide in Him, for He overcame temptation and is able to help us when we face it. **Because he himself suffered when he was tempted, he is able to help those who are being tempted.** (Hebrews 2:18)

Though our Lord was sinless, He was still tempted. The devil tries to make us disobey God. Being tempted by that thought you have isn't a sin of itself; it is when you *give in* to it that you sin. The temptations of Jesus simply proved that He was the perfect sinless Son of God. Jesus understands temptation, and He used His knowledge of the Bible to resist. Jesus, the man, did not sin because He soaked Himself in the word of God, and He depended completely upon His Father. We need to follow our Lord's example, soak in the Scriptures and be faithful in prayer.

Therefore, since we have a great high priest who has gone through the heavens, Jesus the Son of God, let us hold firmly to the faith we profess. For we do not have a high priest who is unable to sympathise with our weaknesses, but we have one who has been tempted in every way, just as we are – yet was without sin. Let us then approach the throne of grace with confidence, so that we may receive mercy and find grace to help us in our time of need. (Hebrews 4:14-16)

<u>Faithful together</u>

I have spoken of the importance of prayer elsewhere but repeat that our prayer life is something to be guarded. We must pray to keep our relationship with our Father alive. Reading the Bible regularly – and not just your favourite bits but the whole of the Bible read right through once a year – keeps us in tune with God. The reality is that we will struggle with our personal prayer and Bible times because not only does life chuck all sorts at us, but the devil will also try to prevent us from drawing from the source of life.

This is why belonging to Church – the people of Christ – is so important. Church isn't just a place you go to on a Sunday to hear a sermon and sing songs. It is much more than that. Before I became a Christian, I used to think that you could be a Christian and not go to church. Then someone spoke to me about how Jesus draws us to a church so we can be supported by each other in our Christian lives.

In my home, I have an open fire where we burn logs and coal that give a cheery glow in the depths of winter. A curious thing happens to a piece of coal that is glowing red-hot when it is taken away from the other pieces of coal – it stops glowing and cools down very quickly. The piece of coal needs the other pieces to keep it alive and glowing. That is what church should be for us. We should be helping to keep each other glowing by meeting and supporting each other regularly and not just on Sundays. Praying with another Christian is one way of remaining faithful.

When our prayer life grows cold, the fire of faith goes out and we become merely religious church attendees on a Sunday. Our church attendance will suffer when we neglect prayer because we will see no point in meeting with the body of Christ when our relationship to the Head is no longer vital. Attend the prayer meeting in your church (if there isn't one, start one!)

If you don't have a prayer partner already, let me encourage you to get one. Meet regularly with someone you can trust. Never partner with someone of the opposite sex (unless it's your husband or wife) because prayer is intimate. We make ourselves vulnerable and reveal a lot about ourselves when we pray, so meet someone of the same sex to avoid temptation. But what if you are a Christian who struggles with same sex attraction and you agree with the teaching of the Bible? Meeting someone of the same sex for prayer could put you at the risk of being tempted to sin.

In that situation it's best to meet with a married couple, who are mature in their faith and understand your dilemma. The Church is a family, so "older" brothers and sisters should welcome and nurture those who are same sex attracted but are clearly being transformed by Christ Jesus – better still, make them part of your own family.

You and your prayer partner must keep the confidence and be honest with each other about the things you struggle with. My prayer partner helps keep me right, and we support one another. **But you, dear friends, build yourselves up in your most holy faith and pray in the Holy Spirit.** (Jude verse 20) **Let love and faithfulness never leave you; bind them around your neck, write them on the tablet of your heart.** (Proverbs 3:3)

Chapter Seventeen

The Perfect Match of Gentleness

and Self-Control

But the fruit of the Spirit is...gentleness and self-control. (Galatians 5:22) We have arrived at the last two qualities of the fruit of the Spirit. Gentleness and self-control are qualities perfectly matched. It is difficult to imagine a gentle person losing their temper and being prone to fits of rage. The bad-tempered are not known for being gentle.

We have all been guilty of losing control at one time or another. And I am all too aware that I have failed many times in this area, especially as a younger man. It is a great encouragement to know that the true Christian can draw upon their God-given ability to control their emotions, desires, and actions to exercise the gentleness of the Lord Jesus.

Gentle Jesus meek and mild?

We, in the twenty-first century, struggle with the concept of gentleness because we mistakenly associate it with weakness. The idea of being meek and gentle means one is weak and ineffective; this is a false understanding of gentleness. The term, 'Gentle Jesus, meek and mild', is avoided because of its association with weakness. I blame artists for the misrepresentation of Jesus Christ. Not all artists, just those like the painter of 'Suffer the children', I saw once. This depicted a group of white middle-class children gathered around an effeminate man with blues eyes and long flowing blond hair, who resembled a woman with a beard.

In overemphasising the quality of love and gentleness of God, we have neglected the complete picture of God's revealed character. In the past, preachers stressed God's justice and wrath at the expense of His mercy and love. Today, many can't accept that the God of love is also the God of Justice and will judge wicked people. There are people who can accept the Jesus who welcomed children, was gentle, kind, and died in weakness upon a cross, but they reject the Jesus who cleared the Temple, cursed the fig tree, and who will return as the judge of all the earth. We must preach the full picture of who God is and not neglect any aspect of His holy character.

Jesus was not weak, but He *was* meek and gentle. The phrase, 'gentle Jesus, meek and mild', is not a quote from the Bible but a hymn. I didn't know the hymn and thought it was a product of sugary Victorian sentiment. I was greatly surprised when I discovered that it was written in the 18th century by one of the world's greatest hymn writ-ers, Charles Wesley.

Wesley wasn't a man known for sentiment but for beau-tiful poetry expressing the evangelical teachings of the re-vival he and his brother, John, were part of at the time. Charles' hymns are full of references or direct quotes from Scripture, and this is the case with 'gentle Jesus,' which may have been influenced by a saying of the Lord Himself. **"Come to me, all you who are weary and burdened, and I will give you rest. Take my yoke upon you and learn from me,** *for I am gentle and humble in heart,* **and you will find rest for your souls. For my yoke is easy and my burden is light."** (Matthew 11:28-30)

Gentle Jesus, meek and mild,
Look upon a little child,
Pity my simplicity,
Suffer me to come to Thee.

Fain [willingly, gladly, eagerly] I would to Thee be
brought;
Gracious Lord, forbid it not;
In the kingdom of Thy grace
Give a little child a place.

Fain [willingly, gladly, eagerly] I would be as Thou art;
Give me Thy obedient heart:
Thou art pitiful [full of pity and compassion] and kind:
Let me have Thy loving mind.

Let me above all fulfil

God my heavenly Father's will;
Never His good Spirit grieve,
Only to His glory live.'

(Charles Wesley 1704-88)

Jesus describes Himself as being gentle and humble. He invites those burdened with sin and trying to be right with God through their own efforts, to come to Him. He is merciful and in Him, we find rest and peace with God the Father. We are to learn from Him and follow His example of humility and kindness. Obeying Jesus is easy and light in the sense that the child of God delights to do His will. Only those who humble themselves and come as children to Christ can receive the joy of knowing Him like this. **"I tell you the truth, unless you change and become like little children, you will never enter the kingdom of heaven. Therefore, whoever humbles himself like this child is the greatest in the kingdom of heaven."** (Matthew 18:3-4) Children, especially little children, are dependent and it's this dependence that characterises true faith in God.

This is the meaning that Wesley has captured in his poem, which is a prayer of the humble sinner, asking for mercy from the person who is not cruel, arrogant, or aggressive but ready to show mercy. It is a prayer to become like Christ, imitating His obedient humility and living to the glory of God. Gentleness, humility, kindness, and meekness are synonyms; they express similar ideas and are essential qualities of a true Christian. Sin is pride, self-reliance, and independence from God. The proud and self-reliant will never accept that they need God at all; so, to be a Christian you need to have humility or meekness, which is an inner attitude to oneself; a realisation if you like, of knowing that in me there is nothing to be proud of. Only the meek will fall at the cross of Christ and beg for mercy, which is why Jesus said: **"Blessed are the meek, for they will inherit the earth."** (Matthew 5:5)

Gentleness is this lowly attitude put into practice. Gentleness is similar to kindness. Christ's gentleness is seen in the way He cared for the sick, the poor, the outcasts of society, the elderly, and the young. Observe how He dealt with the fearful, the weak, and the despairing, and yet this same person is a man of great authority. Jesus commanded demons to flee, and they fled. He ordered the wind and the waves to cease their uproar, and they obeyed. With a word, He healed diseases, raised the dead, and silenced His enemies.

Jesus displayed righteous anger at the cruel stubbornness of the religious leaders when they objected to Him healing on the Sabbath. **He looked round at them in anger and deeply distressed at their stubborn hearts...** (Mark 3:5a) When the occasion called for it, Jesus was angry at sin. He never lost control; He never sinned when angry because He displayed the righteous wrath of God. Twice He dealt with those who desecrated the Temple. John records the first time He entered the Temple and found a noisy market there. They were selling sacrifices for the Passover festival, and because only Jewish currency was allowed in the Temple, Roman coins had to be exchanged. A lot of cheating went on as the marketers overcharged and the money changers clawed in a lot of interest.

Jesus called the market a den of thieves but what upset Him more was that they were meeting in a holy place – a place set apart for the worship of the Almighty.

So he made a whip out of cords, and drove all from the temple area, both sheep and cattle; he scattered the coins of the money changers and overturned their tables. To those who sold doves he said, "Get these out of here! How dare you turn my Father's house into a market!" (John 2:15-16) The Lord Jesus was a man of authority and power, a true man and certainly not weak.

But Jesus was also gentle and humble in heart, and (I say this with reverence) thank God for that! If He weren't gentle, we would have no chance of being shown mercy. If He weren't humble, He would never have gone to the cross. **Have this mind among yourselves, which is yours in Christ Jesus, who, though he was in the form of God, did not count equality with God a thing to be grasped, but made himself nothing, taking the form of a servant, being born in the likeness of men. And being found in human form, he humbled himself by becoming obedient to the point of death, even death on a cross.** (Philippians 2:5-9 ESVUK)

God the Son is equal to God the Father. From eternity He shared perfect fellowship with the Father and the Spirit. He possessed the power and the glory of the Godhead, and the wonderful love of the Father caused the Son to give up that glory, to make Himself nothing in the eyes of men and humble Himself. He became fully man while remaining fully God. His humility took Him to a shameful, horrendous death as a criminal to rescue you and me from sin and eternal damnation. This is 'gentle Jesus, meek and mild'!

Gentleness within the believer is that child-like quality that will depend upon Christ and show kindness, tenderness, and love to others. **Brothers, if someone is caught in a sin, you who are spiritual should restore him gently. But watch yourself, or you also may be tempted.** (Galatians 6:1) We are to deal gently with brothers and sisters in Christ who sin (knowing that we too can easily fall into temptation) giving them the opportunity to repent and be restored to the Christian community.

Be completely humble and gentle; be patient, bearing with one another in love. (Ephesians 4:2) **Let your gentleness be evident to all.** (Philippians 4:5) **Therefore, as God's chosen people, holy and dearly loved, clothe yourselves with compassion, kindness, humility, gentleness and patience.** (Colossians 3:12) **A gentle answer turns away wrath, but a harsh word stirs up anger.** (Proverbs 15:1) **... pursue righteousness, godliness, faith, love, endurance and gentleness.** (1 Timothy 6:11) An arrogant Christian is a contradiction. A true child of God will be humble and gentle to all.

The self-controlled person is not a slave to sin

Gentleness and self-control go together. A person out of control cares nothing for the consequences of their actions and how they impact other people. In today's society, we hear a lot about freedom to do what we like, but the truth is, outside of a relationship with God our Father, we are not free; we are slaves to sin.

Paul paints a stark picture of the person out of control: **The acts of the sinful nature are obvious: sexual immorality, impurity and debauchery; idolatry and witchcraft; hatred, discord, jealousy, fits of rage, selfish ambition, dissensions, factions and envy; drunkenness, orgies, and the like.** (Galatians 5:19-21a) This is a portrait of raw, untamed sin. The person who lives like this lacks self-discipline and is not free but a slave heading for hell. **I warn you, as I did before, that those who live like this will not inherit the kingdom of God.** (Galatians 5:21b)

When Adam sinned, the human race lost the ability to choose right from wrong and became slaves to a sinful nature, opposed to a holy God. Paul expresses this in Romans chapter seven. **I know that nothing good lives in me, that is, in my sinful nature. For I have the desire to do what is good, but I cannot carry it out. For what I do is not the good I want to do; no, the evil I do not want to do – this I keep doing. Now if I do what I do not want to do, it is no longer I who do it, but it is sin living in me that does it.** (Romans 7:18-20)

How often have you tried to 'turn over a new leaf' or failed at keeping a New Year's resolution? How often have you tried to give up a bad habit or have regretted something you said? How often have you made the excuse that you just couldn't help it, you didn't mean it? How many times have you wished you hadn't watched that film or TV programme and wasted your time staring at a screen?

You know what is right, you want to do what is right, you try very hard to change, but you do the wrong thing despite yourself. That is what Paul is saying, he knew the law of God, he loved the law of God, but trying to live a moral and upright life wasn't enough. **I have discovered this principle of life—that when I want to do what is right, I inevitably do what is wrong. I love God's law with all my heart. But there is another power within me that is at war with my mind. This power makes me a slave to the sin that is still within me. Oh, what a miserable person I am!** (Romans 7:21-24 NLT)

We need to realise how wretched and lost we are when we live as slaves to the sinful nature. Paul cries: **Who will free me from this life that is dominated by sin and death?** Not the United Nations! Not any man-made institutions. No government in the world can sort out the mess – they have tried and keep trying but fail. Nothing human beings can do will change our world for the good. The reason why better education, better housing, more jobs, or whatever scheme we come up with fails is because our deep-seated problems are spiritual – we are cut off from our Creator, and it is only He who can rescue us. **Who will free me from this life that is dominated by sin and death? Thank God! The answer is in Jesus Christ our Lord.** (Romans 7: 24-25 NLT) God has done it through Jesus Christ – He sets us free from the power of sin – the things that control us and ruin our lives.

<u>Saying no to sin</u>

However, He has achieved so much more than setting us free from sin. We are now new creations – children of God

– with the power to choose right over wrong. Before I was in Christ, I could not say 'no' to sin, but now I can! Now I can use self-control and resist temptation. So how do we do that? How do we use self-discipline to say no to sin?

1st Remember what sin is

I know we've talked a lot about this subject, but it's really important that we fully grasp what happens when we sin. As we have seen sin, is essentially rebellion against God. Sin is rejecting God and putting ourselves in His place, where life is all about us. Self-centeredness and pride are the heart of sin. Refusing God by not believing in Him is the outcome of sin. All sin is ultimately against God, even sin committed against each other. When David confessed and repented after committing adultery and murder, he said to God, **Against You—You alone—I have sinned and done this evil in Your sight.** (Psalm 51:4 HCSB) In the letter of James, compromising with the world's views and attitudes is compared to adultery: **You adulterous people, don't you know that friendship with the world is hatred towards God? Anyone who chooses to be a friend with the world becomes an enemy of God.** (James 4:4) By re-membering that sin is hatred against the One we love, the One who loved us and went through Hell to rescue us from it, motivates us to say no to sin. This brings us to remem-bering who you are.

2nd Remember who you are

The Christian isn't someone who simply believes in God – they love Him! They love Him and are not part of this sin-ful world opposed to God. They are on a journey through this life to glory, where God uses the trials of this world to show His reflection. They walk the path Jesus has laid out for them: **"Enter through the narrow gate. For wide is the gate and broad is the road that leads to destruction, and many enter through it. But small is the gate and narrow the road that leads to life, and only a few find it.** (Matthew 7:13-14) Martyn Lloyd-Jones recommend, every morning when we awake, every Christian should say, 'God is my Father, I am His child – a child of the living God – that's who I am.' Remember you are a citizen of Heaven, you are passing through this world and you and I are different from everybody else because we belong to God's family. Tell yourself, 'My ultimate home – the place where I truly belong – is in the kingdom of Heaven. I'm just travelling through this world. Yes, I will be tempted by Satan and my own sinfulness however, I do not belong to Satan, nor am I a slave to sin but I belong to the Lord Jesus Christ, who has died for me and brought me out of the rule of darkness into His kingdom of light.' Start the day with thanking God for the life He has given you and remind yourself that you are now His child, so go into the day with this truth in mind and heart.

You remind yourself of who you are, and sin becomes repellent. You can resist it because your love for Jesus is stronger. You are no longer a slave to sin but a child of God, being re-made into His image. **Dear friends, now we are children of God, and what we will be, has not yet been made known.** Our future state, when we are bodily resurrected from the dead, has not happened yet, but it will be glorious! In this present life, we struggle against sin, but when Christ returns, that war will end, and we will become perfect images of God. **But we know that when he appears, we shall be like him, for we shall see him as he is. Everyone who has this hope in him purifies himself, just as he is pure.** (1 John 3:2-3) The Holy Spirit enables us to exercise self-discipline – to keep ourselves pure – and say no to sin by reminding us of who we are. Another thing the Spirit does is bring Scripture to mind.

3rd Remember Scripture is a powerful weapon

Take … the sword of the Spirit, which is God's word. (Ephesians 6:17 NLT) Scripture is a formidable weapon against temptation. Jesus used it when The Satan tempted Him in the wilderness. He quoted scripture in answer to Satan, and each time He silenced the enemy. (You can read that account in Matthew 4:1-11) If King Jesus needed to do that – the sinless One – how much more must we depend on scripture to resist sin? The Holy Spirit helps us when tempted to sin by reminding us of what the Bible says. This should not surprise us because Jesus told us, the Spirit would do this: **But when the Father sends the Advocate as my representative—that is, the Holy Spirit—he will teach you everything and will remind you of everything I have told you.** (John 14:26 NLT)

Reading the Bible regularly isn't just a discipline, it's a pleasure that always rewards. We need to immerse ourselves in scripture – think Biblically and read it, again and again, to get it into our minds. This is something Jesus would have done from an early age because He, like all faithful Jews, memorised scripture to the point that they could recite large chunks of it. In the next chapter, I will tell you how God used the Bible to help me through a painful journey; by bringing scriptures to mind when I needed them the most.

Here are a few examples of scriptures we can memorise and use to help us say no to sin. **"I made a covenant with my eyes not to look with lust at a young woman."** (Job 31:1 NLT) Job intentionally decided to make a solemn promise, a pact with his eyes, not let them look lustfully at a woman. When tempted this way, the Holy Spirit pops this verse in our minds so we can look away and stop thinking about her. You are watching a film, a TV programme, reading a book, surfing the internet, or reading a paper or magazine, and there are sexual images that you begin to enjoy, so this comes to mind: **"You have heard that it was said, 'You shall not commit adultery.' But I say to you that everyone who looks at a woman** [or man] **with lustful intent has already committed adultery with her** [or him] **in his heart.** (Matthew 5:27-28 ESVUK) We could decide not to watch anything that promotes sin by memorising Psalm 101:3 **I will refuse to look at anything vile and vulgar.** (NLT) It's not only sexual images we need to avoid, but also beware of graphic violence. Watching scenes of violence can desensitise us to the real thing. I remember a movie where a man uses other people to shield himself from bullets, and he was the hero! This sort of violent imagery cheapens human life. When what you see causes you to sin, pray Psalm 119:37: **Turn my eyes from looking at worthless things; and give me life in your ways.** (ESVUK)

You are in a conversation with friends or workmates, and it heads in a sinful direction. Perhaps they talk of sex, or they start gossiping, saying hurtful things about someone else. Perhaps an argument is brewing. To give a powerful witness, walk away from the conversation and remember Psalm 34:13-14: **Keep your tongue from evil and your lips from speaking deceit. Turn away from evil and do good; seek peace and pursue it.** (ESVUK) Memorise the Bible, and God will use it to help you resist sin. Resisting temptation is difficult when you fight alone; that's why we need each other.

4th Remember He has placed us in His family for support

God has purposely put true believers in Christ into His family so that we don't have to struggle with sin alone. We need our brothers and sisters in Christ Jesus. The need can be especially great when we struggle with a persistent sin. Supposing you can't give up pornography, or you easily lose your temper, or you doubt because of a severe time of trial. Whatever the sin you struggle with, seek out a mature Christian to mentor you. When I say mature, I'm not referring to physical age but spiritual maturity – someone who has been where you are and overcome it. My Church encourages older saints to mentor younger ones and urges us to find accountability partners. That sounds scary, but it simply means we meet regularly with someone who will ask the important questions and hold us to account. 'How are you doing resisting such and such?' It's someone we can trust who will keep everything confidential. Someone we know isn't judgemental but sympathetic to our struggle with sin. Someone who will pray with and for you. I've mentored a few young men, sometimes reading a good Christian book together; that tackles the issues we are dealing with. It is always rewarding when you see them overcome sin and grow in their faith.

One of the word pictures in the Bible; describing a believer in Christ, is a soldier. Not soldiers fighting another nation but fighting the war on evil and sin. It doesn't matter how well a soldier is trained; if they are on their own in a battle, their chances of survival are slim. No, a soldier is part of an army – we need fellow warriors to support us. It's great to know that those warriors are our brothers and sisters in Christ – part of a loving supportive family. **And let us consider how we may spur one another on towards love and good deeds. Let us not give up meeting together, as some are in the habit of doing, but let us encourage one another – and all the more as you see the Day approaching.** (Hebrews 10:24-25) A spur is a sharp object used to prod a horse into moving. An accountability partner does the same as they challenge us to move closer to God. It can be painful but worth it. It's all about encouragement – we are meant to encourage one another, which is why being part of a local church fellowship is essential to our growth as Christians.

Self-discipline is all about growing into Christ-likeness

It's a co-operation with the Holy Spirit. He enables us to exercise self-control and become mature in our faith. So far, we've looked at this subject from a negative viewpoint, saying no to sin. However, it can be positive as well. We can discipline ourselves to draw closer to God because the more you love Him, the greater your union with Jesus is, the less you desire to sin. Christianity isn't about a set of 'don'ts' – don't do this, don't do that. It's about a relationship with the Living God – enjoying a love that is so great, it is difficult to put into words. It is so perfect; you gladly leave behind anything that gets in its way.

Paul placed self-control, or self-discipline, as the last aspect of the fruit of the Spirit, not because it's the least but because it's the foundation for the rest. Self-discipline enables us to say no to sin, to choose to love, be joyful in the Lord Jesus, look to Him to experience peace, exercise patience, display kindness to others, show goodness, and be gentle.

Chapter Eighteen

Walking Through Grief –

A Personal Story

So far, in this book, I have tried to be objective; I've looked at the subject without relating too many personal details. This is especially true when I touched on the area of suffering. The reason was to avoid comparison and to show, that to the person who suffers, no matter how big or small their trauma may appear to others, all pain is relevant. God understands this, and so Jesus says to Paul, about his thorn in the flesh, **"My grace is all you need. My power works best in weakness."** (2 Corinthians 12:9 NLT)

But now, my aim is to offer comfort and encouragement to anyone who is suffering, by revealing how God has helped me. This is essentially what Paul says he's going to do with the people in Corinth. **He comforts us in all our troubles so that we can comfort others. When they are troubled, we will be able to give them the same comfort**

God has given us. (2 Corinthians 1:4 NLT) I intend to show how God has helped me in an extremely painful journey of grief. He has done this through people who have displayed His image and also through His word. I have witnessed living mirrors as they have shown the love of God to me.

Surrounded by love

When I began writing Living Mirrors, over 14 years ago, my health was reasonably good. My mother and father-in-law were still alive, and my dear wife was working hard as a headteacher in a local primary school. Since then, life has changed dramatically.

In July 2016 my wife, Joyce, was diagnosed with early-onset Alzheimer's. In February 2019, four days after our eleventh wedding anniversary, my beloved died. Joyce had gone into a care home for respite care, but her condition became worse, and she also had a stroke. So, she was given palliative care and her last week was a peaceful one with her pain being managed. Even though I knew she was dying. Even though I had spent the week beside her every day and night, her death was still a shock. Now it was very real. As I looked at her, I had an enormous sense that Joyce was no longer there. Because she was a true believer in Christ Jesus, I knew she was now with Him. However, that didn't stop the pain piercing my heart.

I phoned my care pastor, Andy Jack, to let him know. It was 04:20. He asked if it was okay if he arrived at 06:00. 'Yes, of course', I answered. To my surprise, he arrived twenty minutes later. Andy could not stay at home while a brother in Christ needed him. His support that day went beyond the duties of a pastor. He was Christ's living mirror to me and stayed all day. He was there when I phoned the family to let them know. He called a funeral director whom he knew. I was now in a daze. I didn't know what to do or say. I felt like a lost child. After Joyce's body had been removed, Andy helped me gather her things together. He followed me home in his car. Driving back was difficult. I had to concentrate on the driving and not let the grief overwhelm me. Seeing Andy's car in the rear mirror was a great comfort.

When we arrived at my home, our teaching pastor, Jeremy McQuoid, was waiting for us; he took over from Andy while he went for breakfast. Jeremy was so wise and helpful in what he said. He patiently listened while I rambled on. He made sure I had something to eat, though I wasn't hungry. We recalled how a particular verse of scripture encouraged Joyce just four weeks before: **So we are always of good courage. We know that while we are at home in the body we are away from the Lord, for we walk by faith, not by sight. Yes, we are of good courage, and we would rather be away from the body and at home with the Lord.** (2 Corinthians 5:6-8 ESVUK) Joyce had become very excited when she had heard Jeremy preaching on that text. It was clear that she was looking forward to seeing Jesus and one day being resurrected. I shared how, when she took her final breath, I sensed that she was leaving her body, and I was now being reminded that she was with her Lord Jesus. We acknowledged that this did not lessen the pain; Jeremy described the grief as an open wound, which in time, would become a scar – but I would always miss her. Jeremy left when Andy returned to sit with me. He urged me to have a rest, try to sleep. He would welcome Joyce's sisters who were driving up from Edinburgh. I went to my room. It was full of memories. It was the room Joyce and I shared. I slumped onto the bed and wept. I never managed to sleep; all I felt was raw emotion.

Andy didn't leave until the evening when he knew I was being looked after by Joyce's sisters and my daughter. What I remember most about that week was, in my pain, I was surrounded by love. Though in grief themselves, friends and family helped me with all the practical things I needed to do. It's a cliché but, it's true that I wouldn't have coped without them. The image of God not only shone through His people but also through those who wouldn't claim to be Christians. In my shocked state and intense pain, I was held up by Christ-like love.

Realistic answers?

In chapter 14, I posed the question: How do we know joy and peace in a world of darkness? I made four suggestions. 1. cling to the promises of God. 2. Trust in the purposes of God. 3. Change your perspective and look to Jesus. 4. Pray to be filled with the Holy Spirit.

In the grip of grief, I wondered if what I had written was realistic. Was it correct? Was it too simplistic? My grief made me question a lot of what I had written. The pain was overwhelming. Sometimes I felt as if my physical heart would break in two with an agony I had never experienced before. Death had taken my parents and Joyce's parents – that was hard enough, but this grief felt different. That's because Joyce and I were one in our marriage union. Nothing had prepared me for the depth of anguish I was experiencing. At other times I felt so numb that I could not imagine having peace ever again – or any emotion. Time slowed down. I didn't know what day it was. A day felt like a week. A week like a month. A month like a year. Sometimes grief plunged me into a well of fear. I wasn't afraid, but I felt the sensation and often led me into a flood of tears. I remembered that the Christian writer, C.S. Lewis had also described grief as fear. God felt a trillion miles away – silent to my cries of despair – and yet He was neither absent nor indifferent. He was walking with me in the darkness. He heard every sigh and noted every tear I shed:

You keep track of all my sorrows.
You have collected all my tears in your bottle.
You have recorded each one in your book.

(Psalm 56:8 NLT)

The 'how to' questions in this book are not self-help instructions. They are not directions that, if followed, will improve your life. No, they are practical suggestions to help us focus on the One who can help us. They are a process that the Holy Spirit takes us through. I realised that, without knowing, I was applying these points from chapter 14 to myself. I did cling to His promises, trust in His purposes, change my perspective and pray but not necessarily in that order. Indeed these suggestions are the outworking of faith in God. Because He held on to me and I walked by faith, not by sight, I kept looking to Him for help.

Walking through the valley of the shadow of doubt

On the day of the funeral, I was like a robot, depending on the directions of other people. Once again, I was in the hands of my loving family and caring Church. At the graveside, just moments after Joyce's casket had been lowered into the ground, Jeremy stood behind me and placed his hand on me saying, 'Remember Andrew, that death is the enemy.' He may have added that it was defeated. Death was to blame, not God. Then Jeremy spoke about the resurrection hope of true believers in Christ Jesus. This was not the end but a waiting time. Joyce was in paradise now. One day she will be with Jesus as He returns, and her body will be raised from the dead. I started tuning out. I wondered if those who weren't Christians, listening to those words, would think them a load of nonsense. That the idea of resurrection was farfetched. Then I realised with a shock that *I* was thinking these thoughts. I was doubting what I had believed in for over forty years. I couldn't grasp the hope that Joyce is with the Lord, and this was not the end. As I stared at her casket in the ground, death was so overpoweringly real that it drowned out all thoughts of a brighter future. I was literally hopeless. I didn't feel that it was true. It was difficult to imagine that I would see her again because of the intense agony, fear, confusion, and separation. I sensed the pain and loss.

I struggled for a long time in this inability to grasp the certainty of the resurrection hope, and yet at the same time, I talked to God, telling Him exactly how I felt. I sobbed, when alone, for a month. When people were with me, I didn't cry, not because I was suppressing the tears, but because their presence gave me strength. But when alone, I knew it was all too true – Joyce had gone. Getting into bed at night was a painful reminder that she was not coming back. I remember praying, 'Lord, I know that she's with you, but she's not with me!' So when well-meaning Christians would say, 'Sorry to hear of your loss but praise God she's with the Lord,' that didn't help because I was in a fog, trying to grasp the truth I'd always known but now eluded me, simply due to the intense pain I felt. Believing the Bible does not mean that we do not mourn or feel the loss of a fellow human being. Indeed, as Jeremy, Andy, and others pointed out to me, the more you love someone, the more keenly you will feel their absence. It can be especially tough if you live on your own, as I do now.

As the weeks progress, those who aren't personally affected by grief tend to move on and forget that those close to the person who has gone, are still grieving. Grief doesn't go away overnight. I began to hate the question, 'how are you?' It's usually asked without expecting an answer. I soon learned who I could share with and who not to tell my real feelings to. But God had His living mirrors come to me. Like the man in church who had lost his wife many years before. 'People kept telling me that she was now with the Lord. I knew that, *but she's not with me*, is what I thought.' Those were my words! I had prayed them weeks before, and here was someone who understood exactly how I felt – I wasn't alone in feeling as I did. Other people who had lost someone would approach me sometimes, never say anything, but you knew they understood.

God's answer in the darkness

If we believe that when a true believer in Christ Jesus dies, they are with Him and are now free from pain and full of joy, why do we still grieve? In his message at the funeral service, Jeremy gave the answer. He preached on John chapter eleven, which recounts the raising of Lazarus, a friend of Jesus. Jeremy made two points from the chapter: In the face of death, Jesus weeps with us. In the face of death, Jesus triumphs for us. (I can remember this sermon because it was recorded, and I often listen to it again.) The second point emphasised Jesus' own words; "**I am the resurrection and the life. Anyone who believes in me will live, even after dying. Everyone who lives in me and believes in me will never ever die.**" (John 11:25-26 NLT) Jeremy emphasised that because of the resurrection of Jesus, those who believe in Him would not die eternally; they too will be resurrected. However, because of the block of doubt in my mind, I didn't take comfort from that. It was Jeremy's first point that spoke a lot to me.

John 11:35 is the shortest verse in the Bible, though perhaps it is the deepest expression of love. It's just two words, and they are, **Jesus wept.** Jesus had lost a friend. He knew what He was about to do; He knew that His friend would walk out of the tomb at the sound of His voice. And yet, Jesus wept. He didn't just shed a few tears – He sobbed, He wailed aloud, He groaned with intense agony, His face was soaked in tears – Jesus *felt* the pain of loss. It was so obvious that He was broken-hearted and in anguish that onlookers noticed. **The people who were standing nearby said, "See how much he loved him!"** (John 11:36

NLT) Jesus identified with the sisters and friends of Lazarus, but He also felt the loss personally. The enemy death had intruded into this world, taking away someone made in His image – and He hated it. Jesus wept for His own grief plus the grief of everyone impacted by death to this present day.

Jeremy looked at me directly during his sermon and said, 'Andrew, when you wept last week when Joyce died, Jesus wept with you. When you weep now, Jesus weeps with you.' These are the words I needed to hear; these words began the healing process. This truth was medicine for a broken heart. It gave me a glimpse into the heart of God. He knows what it is like to lose someone. The Father was bereft of the Son while Jesus hung on the cross, carrying our curse. The Son was bereft of the Father when He cried out, 'why?'

If God the Son wept at the tomb of His friend, we Christians should not expect a fellow believer to 'get over it and move on' when someone dies in Christ. Yes – God has done something wonderful about death – He's triumphed over it, and we will see the final victory when death is defeated forever and will be no more. **Then death and the grave were thrown into the lake of fire.** (Revelation 20:14 NLT) However, in the meantime, as the seasons roll on and people die, God is deeply affected by the death of every soul, whether a believer in Christ or not, who was made in His image. He feels it more than anyone can ever imagine. In the face of death, Jesus weeps with us. It was such a comfort to know that God not only understood my grief, but He also shares it. I can look back now and see how God has walked with me on this journey through grief and how eventually the doubt nagging me; was overcome. And walking is literally what I did.

Walking with God in the valley of the shadow of death

I went out for lots of walks around my home village. This helped push the depression away – and kept me fit! I would walk and talk with Jesus. I recalled Scripture. I sang songs of praise. Old and new hymns came to my mind reminding me of eternal truths. Sometimes I listened to Christian songs on my smartphone. One of them, called 'Look up Child' by Lauren Daigle, put into words how I felt. When I couldn't find the words to pray, I recited Scripture. I memorised some psalms, which are excellent prayers, often expressing deep emotions. My prayer life became less formal, much more real. I would tell God exactly how I felt and what I didn't understand. I was completely honest, sometimes saying things another Christian might cringe at. There was no point in hiding my feelings from God – He knows what I'm thinking, so why hide it?

Later in the year, I bought a newly published book called, *Dark Clouds, Deep Mercy: Discovering the Grace of Lament* by Mark Vroegop. Telling God exactly how hurt, confused, and abandoned we feel, is the starting point for this excellent book that looks at the laments (the cries of despair) in the Bible. I highly recommend it, and I was helped immensely by it, not least in knowing that I was in good company telling God how I felt. This prayer from Lamentations expressed my deep emotions and my faith in God,

...my soul is bereft of peace;

I have forgotten what happiness is;

so I say, "My endurance has perished;

so has my hope from the Lord."

Remember my affliction and my wanderings,

the wormwood and the gall!

My soul continually remembers it

and is bowed down within me.

But this I call to mind,

and therefore I have hope:

The steadfast love of the Lord never ceases;

his mercies never come to an end;

they are new every morning;

great is your faithfulness.

"The Lord is my portion," says my soul,

"therefore I will hope in him."

The Lord is good to those who wait for him,

to the soul who seeks him.

It is good that one should wait quietly

for the salvation of the Lord.

(Lamentations 3:17-26 ESVUK)

I learned from this book that I was following the Biblical principle of turning to God instead of away from Him, expressing the pain, asking for His help, and trusting in His good nature.

One of my frequent prayers was, 'I don't understand why, but I do trust You – I know You are good. I **know that for those who love God all things work together for good, for those who are called according to his purpose.** (Romans 8:28 ESVUK) So, even though I don't get why she died, I know and trust Your purposes.' God kept speaking to me in my darkness. Bible passages would flood into my mind when I needed them the most. I could fill a book with them, but here are a few.

> **The Lord is near to the broken-hearted**
>
> **and saves the crushed in spirit**.
>
> (Psalm 34:18 ESVUK)

This is how I felt – broken-hearted and crushed in spirit, but God *knew*, He understood and was so close to me in this gloomy place, it gave me the light of hope. **And Jesus replied, "I assure you, today you will be with me in paradise."** (Luke 23:43 NLT) I felt God was telling me *this is where Joyce is now – in Paradise with Jesus.* **"Do not be afraid. I am the First and the Last. I am the Living One; I was dead, and behold I am alive for ever and ever! And I hold the keys of death and Hades."** (Revelation 1:17-18) This made me think of what Jesus meant by holding the keys of death. Surely it means that His resurrection has defeated death. He has power over it. The jailor has power over the prisoner – he holds the keys – Jesus will, one day, lock up death forever! As I struggled to grasp this truth, I prayed, **"I do believe, but help me overcome my unbelief!"** (Mark 9:24 NLT)

One good indication that God is telling you something and making sure you listen is that He keeps bringing up the issue. In my case, He wanted me to trust Psalm 23. I lost count of the times this psalm was brought to my attention. It kept coming up in conversations, books, a three-sermon series, and even on the radio when I tuned to Classic FM, they were playing a version of Psalm 23. This carried on for well over a month. One morning after it was preached on, a woman from my church offered to lend me a copy of a book called, *A Shepherd Looks at Psalm 23* by Phillip Keller. I turned the offer down – I was reading a lot of books. But God was insistent. On the following Wednesday, another lady from the church phoned to ask me if it was okay for her to send me a book – yes, you've guessed it - *A Shepherd Looks at Psalm 23*! This time I accepted the offer. It was an extremely helpful book. I said to the Lord, 'I get it! I get it! You are *my* shepherd. You are with *me* even though I don't feel it, I get it!' I knew He was with me in the darkness. After this, I memorised that psalm. And then all the mentions of psalm 23 stopped. I had listened and trusted even though the fog of doubt had not completely cleared.

Grasping the truth

One day, Andy related to me something his three-year-old daughter had said. His wife explained that though I would be visiting them, Joyce wouldn't because she had gone to be with Jesus in Heaven. This little girl said in reply, 'Mummy, I'm so glad Joyce is with Jesus because I didn't like seeing her so poorly.' My heart was warmed by that simple faith. I began to picture Joyce with Jesus. I needed this simple child-like faith back. In May the headstone was placed by Joyce's grave. I was going to write, *Joyce A Hill… died 5th February 2019,* but that didn't feel right; I needed to exercise faith, so, eventually, I wrote this instead, *went to be with Jesus 5th February 2019.*

One of the psalms I committed to memory was Psalm 84. It's a prayer about living with God during our journey through this life. Though it talks of the temple in Jerusalem as God's dwelling place, I knew that heaven is where God is because Jesus said, **"Let not your hearts be troubled. Believe in God; believe also in me. In my Father's house are many rooms. If it were not so, would I have told you that I go to prepare a place for you? And if I go and prepare a place for you, I will come again and will take you to myself, that where I am you may be also."** (John 14:1-3 ESVUK) This was another Bible passage God reminded me of, so when I was on a walk and reciting psalm 84, **How lovely is your dwelling-place, O LORD Almighty!** (Psalm 84:1) It wasn't the image of the temple in Jerusalem that came to mind, but God's house in Heaven, where Jesus has prepared a place for those of us who trust in Him. When I recited this: **Blessed are those who dwell in your house; they are ever praising you.** (Psalm 84:4) A wonderful picture pierced the darkness and washed over me with delight. I pictured Joyce, not bent over double by disease, not confused anymore, and not suffering with dementia. Instead, she was standing in the presence of her Saviour. Her face radiant, glowing, full of joy and praising Him. At last, I grasped the truth. She was with Jesus and one day will be resurrected. It wasn't that quote alone, but the combination of all that God had been teaching me and reminding me through this journey of grief.

Missing someone is an expression of love

Did this mean I stopped mourning? That I stopped being sad? That I stopped missing her? Not at all. It meant that I was trusting completely again. God had given me the peace of Jesus in the knowledge that He was with me and my beloved was with Him. Then on one of my walks, He assured me that I would meet her again. I had cried out aloud, 'Lord, I want her back!' And I meant it. Immediately these words came to my mind – there wasn't an audible voice – it was my voice, but it was clear this thought came from God. 'She can't come to you, but you will go to her.' These words echo King David. When his baby had died, he said, **"I shall go to him, but he will not return to me."** (2 Samuel 12:23 ESVUK)

During this struggle, I became aware of the danger of forgetting that the focus of Heaven is God. My desire above all must be to see Jesus and enjoy unbroken fellowship with Him. It would be very easy to make the memory of Joyce into an idol, to want to be reunited with her so much, I would forget that Heaven is where God is. Jesus taught me that seeing Him should be my focus, being with Him, my heart's desire, and meeting Joyce again will be a bonus.

I also learned on this journey that joy and sorrow can exist at the same time. We have joy in the hope of resurrection, yet it is right and proper to miss those we've loved. I met Victor, who lost his wife ten years before. He told me

271

that, even now, after many years, a picture, a place could still bring on the floods of tears. He compared death – especially that of a spouse, whom we were one with – to losing a limb, like a leg or an arm. At first, the loss is devastating. The whole of life as you knew it has been turned upside down, as you try to cope without something that was part of you. You find it hard to believe that the limb has gone, especially because the nerve endings in your body play tricks on your mind, and you can still feel that it is there. You wonder if ever you will cope with life now. But eventually, you learn to adapt to life without the limb – you learn to live a different way. As you gain new skills, you are able to reach out to others like you and identify with them. Life will go on, but you will always be aware that part of you is missing and will not return.

How much we miss someone reveals how much we loved them. 'Grief is the last act of love we can give to those we loved. Where there is deep grief, there was great love.' (Anonymous) If you are grieving or know someone recently bereaved, don't expect life to return to normal. Someone precious, someone made in God's image, has left this world, and they will always be missed. Until our Lord Jesus returns, death and other forms of suffering will be part of our earthly life. As we await that day, let us value every human being, whether young, old, weak, disabled, poor, whatever colour and background. Let us resist the evil notion of today's secular world, that a person only has value because of what they can contribute to society. Let us be living mirrors and love everyone made in God's image.

Conclusion

In the first part of this book, we looked at who God is, His amazing nature, and what He has done to rescue humanity from the devastating effects of sin. In the second part, we saw that God is seen in His children, who produce evidence that the Holy Spirit lives within them. Whenever we look at the God of the Bible and consider what it is to be a true believer in Christ Jesus in this fractured world, a question always arises, if God is love, why is there still suffering? What is He doing about it? I have tried to address that question, not only by teaching about His rescue plan through Christ Jesus and His conquering of death through the resurrection but also by showing that He created a family – a family we call the Church.

Every true believer in Christ Jesus is connected to one another. In a mysterious way, the Church is Christ's body – His representatives on earth until He returns. We don't always get it right because of our struggle with sin. But when we get stuck into the mess of this world, when we get our hands dirty and display Christ's love to everyone in need, even enemies, we make a real difference to those who are suffering. God works with and through His living mirrors, who reflect His loving image.

Appendix: A Poem About Loss

Below is a poem I wrote two years after Joyce died. It's a statement of faith and I hope it helps anyone suffering grief.

By Your Side

O pain my heart has pierced,
As death has come my way
And taken a beloved
Whom I will not see today.

But You, my King Jesus,
You do weep with me.
You hear every sigh,
Every tear, do You see.

It was on the cross You took our sin,
And died in our place.
It was there that God pardoned us,
And displayed His amazing grace!

Jesus' heart was pierced with pain –
His tender heart was broken.
Bitter words of anguish spoken.
Then with a final breath, He gave Himself up to death.

But the Son of God was without sin,
So, death could not keep a hold of Him!
And those who trust in Jesus will be,

Raised to life – His loving face they will see!
'With Me, you will be in Paradise.'
This is what you said,
To those who trust in Jesus
On their dying bed.

Although in this valley of weeping,
Death, Your Face does hide.
I and my beloved,
Are always by Your side.

About the Author

Andrew G Hill was born in Buckinghamshire, England in 1958. His father was in the Royal Air Force, so Andrew grew up on various RAF camps. Born with asthma, absences due to ill health, moving to new areas and attending several schools contributed to a poor education. He left school at the age of 15 without qualifications and never went to university. But he became an enthusiastic reader of adventure and science fiction. He had a love for films and bought many books on the subject. When he was 18, he encountered the Lord Jesus in the pages of the Gospels.

That book changed everything. He wrestled for two years with a strong sense of sin. And eventually he surrendered his life to Christ Jesus and knew the cleansing power of the Holy Spirit. He felt God leading him in to pastoral work and to his surprise preaching. ('To say I was pushed out of my comfort zone would be an understatement.') He studied at Cliff College in Derbyshire, where he qualified as a preacher.

In a moment of zeal, he once prayed, "Lord, I will go wherever You want me to go and do what You want me to do." That prayer was answered by a clear call to London and his response was, "I'll go anywhere but there!" But once he went to the London City Mission (LCM) for interviews and a probationary period, it was clear that God had called him to this work. He qualified with the Theological Diploma of the LCM and served as an evangelist, children and school's worker and itinerant preacher on behalf of LCM. He wrote many short stories, lesson plans for RE in schools, and Bible holiday club material. When ill health forced him to leave the work he loved 18 years later, he realised a long held ambition and wrote his first novel.

God brought Andrew to Scotland, where he now lives in Aberdeen. He has written two "kidult" books of Christian Fantasy: "George and the Monster Inside", "George and the Sinister Shadow" under the name of A G Hill. He is a member of Deeside Christian Fellowship Church in Milltimber, Aberdeen. (DCFC)

He does voluntary work in various ministries at DCFC, including a prayer support team, home group leader, pastoral visitor, missions committee and itinerant preacher. He volunteered to work at Equip Bookshop in Bridge of Don, Aberdeen (formally CLC) and says, 'It's a bad idea putting a book lover in a bookshop and giving him a generous discount!' As a result he has more books than shelves to put them on. Other hobbies include listening to classical music (and having more CDs than shelves to put them on) walking, and cooking (But not at the same time).

'Without Jesus Messiah in my life, I am nothing and can do nothing, so to God be all the glory.'

Some Helpful Books For Further Reading

A Shepherd looks at Psalm 23 W Philip Keller Zondervan Publishing

Surprised by Jesus Dane Ortlund Crossway Publishing

Gentle and Lowly by Dane Ortlund Crossway Publishing

Surprised by Hope Tom Wright SPK Publishing

The Amazing Cross Jeremy & Elizabeth McQuoid IVP Publishing

The Case For Christ Lee Strobel Zondervan Publishing

The Pilgrim's Progress Updated Edition John Bunyan Aneko Publishing (There are many editions of this best seller. Some are in the original 17th century language some updated or edited for modern readers.)

Hope in Times of Fear, The Resurrection and the meaning of Easter Timothy Keller Hodder & Stoughton Publishing

My Rock My Refuge A Year of Daily Devotions in the Psalms Timothy Keller and Kathy Keller Hodder & Stoughton Publishers

The Good God Enjoying Father, Son and Sprit Michael Reeves Paternoster publishing

Being There How to Love Those Who Are Hurting Dave Furman Crossway Publishing

Dark Clouds Deep Mercy Discovering the Grace of Lament Mark Vroegop Crossway Publishing

Side by Side walking with others in wisdom and love Edward T Welch

How to Talk About Jesus Without Looking Like An Idiot Andy Bannister IVP books

Enjoy Your Prayer Life Michael Reeves 10 Publishing

Holiness J C Ryle 10 Publishing

The Lord's Prayer Kevin Deyoung Crossway Publishing

Tumbling Sky Psalm Devotions For Weary Souls Matt Searles 10 Publishing

Growing in Christ J I Packer Cro

George and the Monster Inside A G Hill Independently published available on amazon

George & The Sinister Shadow A G Hill Independently published available on amazon (It's bit cheeky recommending my own books but the first explores forgiveness and second includes a look at loss and grief)

Printed in Great Britain
by Amazon

b6faf4a2-bc56-4e19-adbc-b2bb14407b07R01